Contents;

Part 1 Coming To Terms

5/ My life in general
8/ Where did it all go wrong
36/ The calling & after the calling

Part 2 coming to terms

44/ My friends
46/ When to give up
47 The social drinker
48/ The regular drinker
50/ The binge drinker
51/ The top up drinker to a serious problem
55/ The full blown alcoholic

Part 3 Giving up day by day

58/ A new beginning step by step day by day
60/ A regular drinker
63/ When to give up
64/ Day one of giving up for the regular drinker
72/ Helping and understanding the full blown alcoholic
76/ Freedom from hell !!!

To Linda all the best

[signature]

7 2 2016

This compelling and true life story of the author taking you through a very troubled life which led him to become a full blown alcoholic with only days to live, to survive this terrible illness, by way of a very powerful, spiritual happening, A DIVINE INTERVENTION.

The contents of this very moving book will help anyone in any stage of this terrible illness to give up the booze forever, and like myself, embark on a whole new life without the bottle, for a life you may not have known existed other than your hell hole you are now in.

Published by H.Harman
H.Harman@sky.com
Author : A.E.Marchant

INTRODUCTION

First of all. picking up this book is, without doubt, the admittance that you have a problem, and yet the bottle is still your friend; you cannot let go of it; you may see no life without it either; the list of reasons to regard it as a friend can be endless.

Congratulations, this is your first step to recovery! Also, by picking up this book I would like to make it clear that the contents may be, at times, disgusting to read, but all the contents are very true.

My reason for writing this very true book is to not help you give up the booze, but for you to give up the booze and free yourself of your so called friend, to see it as a false friend, who will kill you in the end. You may ask yourself who is this man telling me how to give up? What authority does he have to help me? My authority is that I am one in over 50, 000 who was told that I would not last another week if I did not stop drinking. This gives me a good reason to help you to survive just like I did; together we will understand each other to a given end, page by page. I will become your friend. Nothing will give me more reward than the feelings of success in your success to beat the bottle.

The road forward is not easy, but with faith and hope this can all be possible.

I am not here to just say 'give up the booze' like people, who do not understand this terrible addictive illness may do. Not a single person, who has not become a victim of this addiction, this obsessive illness can comprehend the sometimes suicidal and despairing feelings of having no hope for oneself. Feeling so ill, and yet still wanting to do anything to get another drink. The withdrawals from one drink to the next one is only known by those who are in this terrible state or have been through it themselves. Not even the medical profession understands the absolutely horrific and confusing feelings of withdrawal either. As I have said, you have to be in it to understand that this is the key to the door, this is what makes us relate with others in the same state of affairs themselves.

As for myself, I will, in the following pages, explain my life to you and what lead me to become a full-blown alcoholic, even though I had previously drunk socially and modestly for 40 years. Some readers may find the contents of this somewhat disgusting at times, but it is the truth. If the truth hurts or even offends you in any way, read on for your own future benefit, that you may have a chance to beat this illness before you get to the full blown stage, maybe of no return. Alcohol is subtle and insidious - many drink and do not realize that they are already in fact alcohol dependent.

I did not write this informative book to fill your head with health charts either, drink units or other problem units that doctors use to try and show how they understand. You know that ultimate and disgusting and degrading death is the only result to go by. I know that I was saved from impending death for the benefit of others, and I am sure that if you believe in me and believe in yourself and also let the Higher Power enter your life, you can beat the devil forever
from the so called friend who is hiding in the bottle. Face it, I am still here to write this book, but will you still be here to read it?

MY LIFE IN GENERAL

My life of drinking was no different, I suppose really, to any other adolescent in the early 1970s. Getting pissed on a Friday night and saying on Saturday morning 'never again' till the next time, was commonplace. Although I did not come at all from a family of drinkers, it seemed to be the social norm to me amongst my contemporaries somehow.

Having come from a very strict family, my very early years were a constant array of aggravation and mental turmoil. My mother was the devil itself, constantly hitting my father and shouting at him every day. He would never have retaliated as he was a Christian and used to go up to London on the train with his soapbox and put the world to right. I can always remember him saying 'if only I as a person, listened to me say it is still your result'. I never ever saw my father happy; he was never allowed in the front room either. He was confined to the kitchen or his bedroom. My home life was a mess, although I did not know any different. I sat ashamed, wondering if every house or family was like this? It was frightening really.

I never knew what love was, to be kissed goodnight or to have a loving hug. Being a Marchant you were supposed to be strong and keep your inner feelings to yourself at all cost, a cost that even being raped on several occasions was absolute hell, too frightened to even tell my parents. A Marchant being raped was not the thing my parents would entertain for one moment. All this and more besides to some degree left an awful scar on my personality. I could not wait to leave school and leave all this behind me.

I was too frightened to be around people of my own age and I sought the company of people much older than myself This gave me more assurance that in their company nothing would happen to me.

At sixteen I went to college to learn welding and engineering. Disaster struck when I had a serious motorcycle accident that left me mentally scarred and I was in hospital for ten months. On the day of the accident a vicar was called to my bedside and my family was told that I would not last the night. But, survive I did against all odds, for reasons that were not apparent at the time, but became very apparent in later life.

The accident afterwards led me even closer to older people and of course, the pub became a very important part of my life. I felt safe in the pub environment and in the company and drank regularly at the age of sixteen. I always respected drink and never really got pissed up, but looking back it was a relief and a beer or two with the company helped me to get out of my very troubled past. From this time onwards drink became my life. I had found a place of sanctuary, a place where I could get away from home, being surrounded by my new friends. This made the pub my home really, I enjoyed playing pub games, with a drink, and this all made me feel blessedly relaxed after a few pints.

I never put the pub before my work. In fact, the pub became a reason to work hard. The thought of a beer after work seemed like a reward to myself, and in no way was I a budding Alco either, or so I thought.
I got married at twenty-seven and had two daughters and bought my first home. Money was very tight and really I did not push the boat out with booze, although I did drink after work sometimes, but not really any more than most people. I enjoyed drink but in no way was I an alcoholic.

I started my own business and this grew rapidly over the next thirty years of trading, and became very successful, and I never drank during working hours or lunch break in the working week. Like everybody else, I looked to the weekends to relax and enjoy the pub atmosphere, friends laughing, having a beer. This was the way my life had become.

In my late fifties life again became very troubled and stressful, although I had no financial worries and had just bought a small farm and a beautiful house to boot. What could go wrong?

But, let's go back a bit...

I had used drink as a medicine for over thirty years really. It helped me to combat severe depression, which I found out by accident. The day in question I was away on a business trip and came over feeling very ill, in fact, so ill that there was no way of driving any further. I was all over the road and feeling faint and also starting to have a panic attack.

Lucky for me there was a pub and I pulled into the car park and just sat there, thinking of all sorts of things. How was I going to get home? An intense fear also overwhelmed me. Unbeknown to me, as this had never happened to me before, I was having a full-blown panic attack. My heart was thumping and I was hyperventilating and profusely sweating to say the least.

I needed help, so I basically fell out of the car and staggered to the pub door. Again in my life I urgently needed the comfort of others, but not feeling like a drink I remember. Sitting down at a table, the barman could obviously see that I was very unwell, came over *and* started talking to me and asked whether I needed an ambulance. I said that I would rather just sit there for a while if he didn't mind. He offered me a pint of lager, which I drank. The strangest thing was that after finishing that pint my symptoms of feeling ill began to subside very quickly and within half an hour I was feeling as fit as a fiddle, so I had another pint. Now feeling quite normal again I could start to relate back over the whole episode. But, at the time, I did not realize that it was just those two pints that brought about the feeling of normal. Over a period of time I began to see a pattern to the subsidence into depression and feeling unwell and the raising of the spirit and well being every time I had a drink. I'd sussed it. At last I had found a cure for my depression and panic attacks, a solution to my illness was as simple as a couple of drinks; I had found my savoir in all ways.

My depression was often so great that there were times when I staggered to the pub, sometimes even helped to the pub and my close friends would sit me down, get me a pint, knowing full well that I would be fine in half an hour or so. And I must admit that my closest friend ever, big Trevor as he was known, and my brother Nigel, were the only two people who really understood me. My doctor at the time told me that my
four pints a day was ok, but he also said that this could lead to more problems in the future.

What problems, I thought? I've cured **the** problem, and cured the problem I did for thirty years or more using drink very seriously to eradicate my increasing bouts of depression.

But, now back to
WHERE DID IT GO WRONG?

As I have previously said, I was now in my late 50s and was looking forward to semi-retirement in my new life on my small farm after many years of hard work. I had now more time on my hands to enjoy my grounds and keeping the farm looking great. I felt great as well; three days back at my business and the rest of the week to enjoy myself; and enjoy myself I did, or I thought I was enjoying myself....

I suppose it was a time when if it were not true it should have been on East enders.

I hadn't really noticed, but my wife was now drinking quite a lot too: three bottles of wine a day plus beer had become normal for her. My marriage of thirty years was somewhat on the rocks as she became increasingly very unpleasant towards me. She became increasingly verbally nasty to me, to say the least.

I was working the three full days a week in the office, and most of my time at home, working on the farm. She became very bored with being on her own all day and really, I see in retrospect, drank the day's boredom away. Slowly but steadily, all the housework went out of the window, eventually even the cooking so there were no meals to eat, which at the time I felt her actions were aimed specifically at me and it got me rather pissed off, I didn't see or realize her descent into what I now think was full alcoholic dependency .

My depressions became worse and I started needing relief from the home life by drinking before work; by now there was, in fact no way could I do without it; it became more and more my friend, my instant savoir against all the problems which seemed to be mounting against me.

Of course, soon, come ten o'clock, my urge to have a drink actually whilst at work was starting to be more necessary. I would slip out to the local store and always brought back at first just a half bottle brandy and put it in my coffee - a great idea at the time! It was as if in my own mind nobody would know and it seemed to satisfy me to feel normal and allow me to work as usual, and it never seemed to cause any wrong directions in my business. At first the half bottle of brandy would last me the day, topping up my coffee, a great taste with a great wellbeing, but there was concern for my general welfare by my partner and my staff about my drinking. Some days I would go to work early before anyone got there to get some drink down me before they arrived at work. This carried on in the same way for six months or so, and on my days not at work it was not unusual to drink a can straight out of bed instead of coffee. I could not bear the thought of another day with my wife and I seemed to have lost any thoughts of doing anything around the farm either. Some times like this I would drink, then go back to bed; get up and drink again, and go back to bed. Life was now starting to become worse. In no way did I think all my problems were anything to do with the booze; it seemed a safety valve and my only solution - I suppose, a way of easing, if not getting out of this world, a world unbeknown to me that was to get far worse.

I had also, for a short while, been aware that both my close friend Roger and my nephew, Richard were dying of cancer and this was just too much to bear. This was, I think as Churchill once said: "Now this is not the end. It is not even the beginning of the end. But it is, perhaps, the end of the beginning" **(Sir Winston Churchill** *Speech in November 1942 British politician (1874 -1965))*.

Richard was now very ill so it was arranged that I would be taken to his house to see him. I had a drink before going as a form of courage. While I was with him we both drank all afternoon, and bearing in mind I was half pissed before I went I was fairly drunk by the time to go home.

However, for me booze was the only answer to cover my distress at seeing Richard so ill. My only way of coping with this *poxy life* that it had now become. We talked about old times together and our growing up with each other and as Richard was a heavy drinker himself, we even more related with each other all afternoon. I felt deeply upset by the whole affair and took it very hard, as I suppose anyone would. The brandy was flowing, it had to be done in my mind, what a fucking unfair life, and my thoughts were revolving around the repeated phrase in my head *'fuck it, fuck it'*.

What with struggling with myself, my wife and now the awful full realisation of Richard's coming death, life seemed meaningless. Although I never let Richard know what was in my head, I can remember leaving there feeling deeply disturbed and depressed, 'why him and not me?' He, after all enjoyed his life and mine was becoming a mine field of depression and guilt - that terrible feeling of guilt that filled my head. I felt guilty that I was not enjoying life, that I wanted death or something like it to end an increasing dark pit which was my life now. He died; that afternoon became the last time I ever saw Richard and I suppose I felt guilty for that too.

On getting back home from that afternoon with Richard, my wife seemed very off hand and not at all unconcerned about Richard. She was, of course even more unconcerned about myself. She seemed unable to relate to the awful trauma and upset in my head and what I was going through. I was also completely uncaring about the state she had become with her own drinking. I felt deeply depressed and I just wanted to get away from what I saw as her absolute fucking negative ways.

As it was a nice, sunny evening I grabbed a few cans and left the house and went down to the stream and sat there drinking, drowning in my own miseries and depression. I can only say that I felt I had nowhere to go except to wallow in my mind and try to find relief from getting the drink down; the booze was definitely the only answer in life; an answer that to me got me out of this fucking awful mess. I didn't realise it, but I obviously fell asleep there. Unbeknown to me my wife had made a call to the police stating that I had gone to hang myself or harm myself in some way. It is possible that in her alcoholic state, she believed that. But, I didn't see this at the time.

On waking, it was now dark, there was an incredible noise thumping in my head, a helicopter was hovering right above me with a large searchlight blinding me . The helicopter was only about sixty feet over me - but the loud thump of its engines and the blinding flashes of the searchlight terrified me. It was absolutely fear-provoking . I turned my head and became aware of police and dogs barking coming towards me. I did not know what the fuck was going on. To me it was something to escape from. Fuck knows what was going through my head. Somewhere, in my mind I thought they must be looking for the wrong person, an escaped prisoner or killer or something. The noise of the helicopter was horrendous and drove any rational thought from my head. The Police with the dogs were now after me. I scrambled up in panic and ran toward my house, running through thickets and grasses as hoped for cover, anything to get away from them. I made it to the house and burst through the door, only to be amazed by seeing the house seemed full of police and ambulance men.

' You've got the wrong man! What the fuck is going on," I shouted and ran past everyone to my bedroom and locked the door. They started talking to me about the whole episode through the door and I explained that I had fallen asleep by the stream and in no way had I gone to kill myself either. What a fucking day! My wife was then arrested herself for maliciously wasting police time.

But, of course the police wanted my medical records after the event because, being in the gun trade, it is a mandatory procedure to check the state of your mental health and capability to be trusted with firearms. It showed that I was on anti-depressants and also had an alcohol condition as well. So, through the whole episode, this made another change to my life. A change that became even worse as I was not allowed by law to enter my own shop.

I had lost my career as well.

Now with the whole week to myself, my depressions increased and my drinking was now starting to become very severe, although I did not see that there was a problem at all. How could my friend in the bottle, that made me feel better, be my problem? I was also at this time of Richard's death, at a very low ebb. A feeling of complete sadness overcame me like an all enveloping grey blanket, and my depression deepened. The more depressed I became, the more I was needing to drink. It was during this time that it occurred to me that something had to get better, my life could not go on like this. But, you know what these thoughts did, they sent me on to my friend, my only friend in the bottle. How wrong. Things got worse, much worse very quickly.

It was agreed by my business partner that, because of my inability to come to work, and not being allowed in the shop, that I would retire with the understanding that I remain a consultant on full pay, if I were to give him the controlling share. We had always trusted each other as friends and so I could not really see a problem with this so I agreed to sign over my controlling share to my partner. After only what seemed a very short time he sacked me. My friend the booze had made me compound my stupidity

to make the most stupid decision of my life up to then, but in my mind, I would not let the bottle be responsible for the loss of my business, worth at that time over £280 000, all with the drunken stroke of a pen either.
Now I had no income at all. I had lost it, lost everything that I had worked so hard to create for thirty years, all gone.

My marriage was for the same reason, in an agonizing state as well; there seemed no way out; my life was an absolute and virtually complete mess. I was a mess! Then on top of all this the phone rang one morning and I was told that my other nephew, Malcolm, had been killed in a motorcycle accident. I was dazed by this further tragic news. I could not fucking believe it, and I think that that was the last straw to finally tip me over the edge. 1 felt I was verging on being suicidal at the time, and because of my state of health, the further despair that there was no way of going to the funeral as well. 1 felt in a state of absolute despair and in deep, deep depression. I looked in a disreputable disgusting state, maybe even smelling and not washed properly. I could not see that it was the fucking booze!
1 still only saw it that it was a way, the only way of relieving the pain of life and my terrible depressions which could take me to the very brink of suicide.

My life was now on a very rapid decline and - perhaps thankfully, my wife moved out of the house into a caravan on the farm. Now with nobody to relate to at all, the house quickly became a fucking pigsty. I was unable to concentrate to tidy or clean anything. Such things were peripheral to my life to say the least. I needed to concentrate on my depressions and the relief that alcohol gave them, but in less and less easement to my mind. Over the next few months my health worsened rapidly. I was not going shopping or even eating properly and also with living on the farm there were no nearby shops or any way of getting more booze as 1 was too ill to even contemplate driving to town. I remember using taxis to ferry me to the off-license to bring back my *""friend in the bottle, the magic genie in every drop of alcohol"*. -there was no longing for, or even a thought in my head for food - I just lusted for my addiction, *JUST THE BOOZE.*

I was now living in a complete daze, a dream sounds as if it is magical and lovely, but this continuing dream was a constant nightmare, not knowing whether it was night or day sometimes. The floor and any convenient space in the house was completely covered in cans and bottles and at this time I started collapsing at times, waking up in all sorts of dangerous and possibly harmful situations, I had somehow, without clear memory broken my fingers, and my toes and I had really bad bruising all over my body. I was all on my own and in an oddly passive way, looked forward to my possible death.

I had reached a point, a long way beyond the point of any self motivated return. There was no way that I could continue anymore. I had not eaten for weeks I lived on the content of the booze. Even when I tried I was sick on the first mouthful so why keep trying. I had become fucked, truly fucked. It was now impossible for me to even to stand up I was so weak. My drinking had become so severe that there was no relief in time from one drink to the next. The friend was insistent in drinking, but no longer helping me in any way. Yet, even when I had collapsed for a period of time, the first thing I thought of when I came round was to have a drink. The withdrawals when I had no booze in the house were absolutely horrific - I cannot explain what this feels like. It is worse than a complete despair, a horrendous shaking and vomiting, even shitting oneself at the same time and the immense fear of everything one has ever imagined of a burning hell, to which another drink might give relief and stop
this. By now the drink did not give relief but the addiction did not stop, more, more,
more
Of course the time from one drink to the next becomes ever shorter to get even a whisker of relief, my friend now taunted me - my friend was now the Devil himself. Life was now a battle, a battle which I was seriously losing. There was now no way of even getting back to bed. I was just too weak to pull myself up on to it and I remember lying on the floor, shivering and freezing cold amongst all the cans and bottles through that wintertime. As for getting to the loo, well, I had no option, I just pissed or crapped myself where I lay next to the empty cans of booze by you which had promised relief, now all empty laying on the floor - my vanished saviour in a can.

I was in and out of consciousness now all of the time and somewhere inside my head I knew that this was the end. I felt so weak and ill, but something from some deep layer in my consciousness gave me a small, perhaps even urgent voice of survival, the strength to want to somehow survive, and something from some deep recess inside me said: 'Crawl to the phone for help'. I was virtually unable to make any movement. I can recall taking a long and painful time despite all the effort I could muster, to crawl and somehow pull my body nearer and nearer to the phone, but when I got there, I could not stand up or even pull myself into a kneeling position to get to it so I just lay there amongst all the filth and empty cans and bottles and somehow pulled the cord down and then somehow rang 999. I croaked as I tried to tell them my plight. Unbeknown to me it was Christmas Eve, perhaps very apt. I think they thought that I had just had too much to drink that evening or something. I managed in failing consciousness to give them my address and really, that's the last thing I can remember.

The next thing I can remember then was a torchlight shining through the window at me lying on the floor, too weak to move. I could not move to undo the door, so they broke the window to get in - the help I needed was now here. They said that I was totally emaciated and had to go with them. I had an underlying faint feeling of hope. It was such a relief to just see another human being - it gave me an odd but very real feeling of comfort and support which was the start of the journey to an end of all this mess, or so I thought.

The way to hospital was all a blur really as I was in and out of consciousness all the time and did not really know much about it either. All that I knew when I woke up was that I was in a room with no windows, and being examined by doctors. What they thought I do not know, I must have been smelling disgusting, worse than a Pole cat and in a horrendous state of emaciation. I was put on a drip immediately and then the next phase of the living nightmare was beginning to take its course.

I was now without the booze and the absolute fear of being without its support was terrifying, the oncoming withdrawal was already becoming intense. I was shaking all uncontrollably all over my body. It was just too terrible. I actively thought that rather than this, I wanted to die. There are no words to describe the feelings of withdrawal. I don't know how long this went on, but suddenly I decided I could not handle it any longer. All I could think was that I must have my *BOOZE, BOOZE...* that's all I could think of. I pulled out the drip from my arm *and* could only think of one thing. I was driven into thinking 'Get off this bed and get out of this place!'

But, I was emaciated with very nearly no muscle left, so of course, all I could achieve was simply to fall onto the floor physically hurting myself to add to the mental pain. The blood was streaming out of my arm where I had pulled out the drip. Even with all this fear the determination to *GET out* of here to get another drink was overpowering. But, I just could not move anymore; I was *Fucked, Fucked in the head; fucked physically and fucked in the wracking and terribly horrendous addiction withdrawals.* As an added shame, I was now on the floor with the nursing staff rushing to get me back up onto the trolley. They were having difficulty in lifting me, they could not use a hoist as it is not hospital policy to let them do so, only the porter is allowed to use a hoist it seems. As he was not present I just lay there on the floor limp and dripping out of any attempt to lift me. While, after what seemed to be a long time, maybe many hours, I was manhandled the best they could back onto my bed, the drips re-inserted. - fuck knows how long it really was, but it did seem hours to me in my delirious state. *' Why, why do all this? Leave me alone"* was in my head. If I couldn't have my drink, what was the point?. I just wanted to die really - a professional man brought to his knees by the bottle, and yet, to me at that moment, the alcohol was still all that was important. I still stupidly sort after it to help me. It was the most important thing in my life. It was still my friend, my saviour, the one thing that could take away my pain and my depression. It was alone the only thing that could, and would put right everything I was feeling.

As the days passed in the hospital I was confined to a room that also had no windows. All I did was to look at the clock, with no way of knowing night from day, as if that fucking really mattered. I was put on a special liquid diet, as if I tried to eat anything solid, I would spew it up. The drink, I was told was full of goodies for malnutrition and emaciation. It could help to make me strong again until I was well enough to leave. I then thought I would try to get better - that way I could get out and have another quick drink. It would really make things better.

I was still totally confined to my bed, not by choice, but because my body was so weak and my muscles had wasted away. I could not offer a cup up to my own mouth, or even wipe my own backside after using the bedpan. I lay in listlessness. The time somehow shuffling past, minutes into hours, hours into days, days into months.

As the days went past the terrible and hellish withdrawal symptoms became easier and slightly less uncontrollable. Also, the detox pills they gave me did to some degree help with the constant shaking. I was in the isolation ward for about a week then transferred to the open ward that was full of people like me. It had never occurred to me before that so many people were like me, some only 20 years old, looking yellow with all sorts of tubes coming out of them. In some way I was somewhat comforted that I was not the only person on this planet who was suffering from this terrible addition illness.

I suppose we were not the favourite patients, often abusive and unhelpful. Perhaps because of this, the staff did not always treat us as well as they should have. Some were spiteful and were sometimes downright nasty towards us, with the attitude that we were responsible for the state of ourselves and that this illness, this terrible
addictive illness was self-inflicted. Which, I suppose in a way it was. at least at the start. Until the alcohol took over all control of us. There was also no apparent concern for our wracking withdrawals. For me, just as an added bonus being a smoker did not help at all either. Many times I would just break down in tears of complete and utter anguish.
Talking to the hospital vicar helped; anything to take away the constant thought of what he referred to as the hellish burden of that *devil-drink*, although I said nothing, but in my mind alcohol was still my saviour friend.

As the weeks passed in what became my 5 weeks stay in hospital, I was seen by all the services you could think of Social Services were involved in my case so as to ascertain what would be my future once I left the hospital. There was nobody to look after me, not even my own wife, when I got home.

I was now, after about four weeks, on a Zimmer and was starting to be able to walk and keep food down, but I could do nothing more for myself really. So after five weeks in the hospital it was agreed that Social Services would come to my house every day to help with my after care.

But. now with all sorts of troubles in my mind including that of having no access to money, I just did not know which way to turn. It was agreed I join a walk-in drink Clinic, a type of Alcoholics Anonymous, to talk to just talk to others who were hopefully surviving, and to some degree it helped in knowing that I was not on my own in this effort to remain alcohol clear.

It is a terrible mess in fact, to share one's own feelings with others who could relate to yourself. It was, however, very rewarding to know people were out there who I did not know existed, who made it a less lonely place to be in.
Although I had not had a drink for five weeks in hospital or had a smoke either, just being home and to have a fag was, to some degree, a great relief. My benefit money by this time had been sorted out, which was a great relief too. However, life was not good.

I was still waking up in the night, sometimes shaking and sweating. I was actually dreading the morning. The start of a new day was just too much to handle, I had nothing to look forward to, and I was wracked with very strong thoughts of suicide crossing my mind. I was trapped in a living hell, thinking of every and all negative things. There was still depressions. There seemed to be no way forward. All that I had ever achieved in my life was now finished, all gone. My solace with my sanctuary in the pub and with all my drinking pals - that too was a thing of the past and gone. What had been my whole life, the way out of depression and negative thoughts in the drinking environment, the only place where I had considered that I had the happiest moments in my life, was now gone.

And, of course, my severe depressions worsened with no way of controlling them with Drink, the way I had done for so many years. What the fuck was I going to do? It was starting to get beyond a fucking joke, waking every day to a living hell - it was like having a serious hangover and severe addiction withdrawal 24 hours a day.
My darling wife was not making it easy for me either. She was still what I realise now as being heavily alcohol dependent and seemed to not care when drinking in front of me. She, perhaps because of her need, which in retrospect I realise had been a selfish need in me too, meant she had absolutely no thought of my wellbeing at all. She just took the piss out of the whole situation. It was too devastating. A situation that I just could not

handle any longer, *and I mean no longer*. Fuck life! What life? Fuck the world really. My friend in the bottle was just there, so near, I could smell it, my friend, my best friend ever who would take all the depression and my 24-hour pain and withdrawal hangover away. Remove all the pain in such a quick and easy way.

I succumbed to the devil. I opened a bottle and could not get it down my throat quickly enough. The relief was absolutely astounding! I suddenly felt free of withdrawal pain and depression. Now, I again I had my depression under control. Now I felt I was in control of my life again with no thoughts in my head of the stupidity or the danger, or that I would with that drink, probably, if I was lucky, return to the hospital. Or that if I wasn't lucky, I had again put myself back onto the slide into the pit of oblivion and ultimate death. I'd been there, seen it done and yet it did not impress me to stop. It was on my mind and I thought that in no way would I allow myself to go back to that level. Just a couple of beers to ease the pain, was all I wanted. In fact, I did believe that the fear of being back in hospital with no booze or fags would keep my drinking under some control.

My marriage was again at breaking point. The immense love I had all my life held for my wife was fading. We were now both heading in the same direction with drink, but not together. The new life I had now found with the bottle was starting to make a serious change; a change for the worse; my friend had deserted me yet again; I was quickly back where my friend who made me feel better had now again become my demise. I quickly dropped down to not eating or bathing, it was not long before I was back where it started before and I was sliding to become a pitiful disgusting creature. Social Services saw the sudden decline and arranged that I be admitted back into hospital yet again, and as the ambulance arrived the thought of no booze or fags was the only thing on my mind, the only important thing on this planet to me was the next drink.

I think the second time in hospital was acutely worse than the first time as I knew what to expect: the absolute anguish, the immense boredom, the terrible craving. The staff said to me: 'What! You again!' My bad treatment by some of the non-caring nurses who did not understand the addictive illness, was beyond belief All the usual things again, including nappies as I had constant diarrhoea and I think the nurses not unnaturally got pissed off with me as I kept asking for a bedpan, and again I was too weak to walk anywhere. My whole body was covered in sores, I looked like a fucking leper with yellow skin. My long hair was just a matted mess, I was again laying for hours and days just staring at the ceiling.

By now there was concern about my welfare, mentally and physically. My wife admitted that she wanted me to be sectioned under the mental health act, but Social Services said that this was not to be the case. Also, the doctors agreed to this and my wife's request was refused. My stay the second time in hospital was not as long as the first time. It was about four weeks and again by eating and all sorts of body building drinks, I was helped and the day of coming home arrived although I needed a walking stick to help me walk and could not dress myself either. So coming home was again a nightmare.

Not being able to shop for food was a great problem and also, my wife refused to cook and again moved out of the house and started to live in a caravan on the farm. The Social Services were very helpful, knowing full well what was going on, but really, what more could they do.

My immediate family were no help either. I was on my own yet again. All sorts of things were happening to me. I was again going to the Health Clinic and also seeing Mental Health consultants. But my slow gains were destroyed when I found my wife in the bam with a rope around her neck, standing on a chair; this started to change my life again. I rang the police and told them about finding my wife, but they seemed more interested in me and my plight than helping my wife, as if I was having delusional visions and dreaming it all.
Later, she admitted her actions and did not deny it to them. I think in general the whole medical profession,. Social Services and the police were absolutely fed up with me. and her too.

My need for food was very apparent as there was no way of going to the shops, so I got in touch with a shop that would deliver door to door. It seemed a great way forward: my food and my fags being delivered, or so I thought. The man delivering my goods became somewhat of a friend, a friend in lambs clothing. It was ok to start off with, but of course my wife was also getting him to bring booze for herself He knew of my condition of being an alcoholic trying to get off the booze.

Looking back I realise he was only thinking of pound notes and his business profits really and it was not long before I was tempted by his suggestion that he could bring me a few cans of beer each week. My mind and body just wanted more of the fucking stuff and the yearning for it was getting worse than before.

From opening the first can and gulping it down I felt the need increasing. Within days I was back well on the road of destruction. I needed more and more. The more I drank, the more he would supply me, even though he knew of the danger of my serious drinking addiction. It did not matter in the least to him, I no longer cared about the cost of the beer, and he was lining his pocket. It even got to the stage where he, because I was again getting incapable, was actually getting me out of bed and placing me in a chair to drink.

By now my health was yet again racing downhill. I was struggling to even lift the can up to my mouth without his assistance. Such a helpful friend, it seemed, but in clear hindsight as I look back, I realise that he did not give a fuck about me at all, only his financial gain - he was probably swindling me as well as feeding me more and more alcohol. He would also fill in my chequebook and make me sign it for the next delivery of booze. But of course back then, the booze that he brought me was my saviour and he was my great friend and helper to my total addiction.

As the weeks passed nothing seemed to changed except my health. I was now bedridden, virtually rotting in my bed, lying in my own piss and shit and yet he still continued to bring more booze for my wife and then coming into the house to dose me up again.

It takes some fucking believing really, but it is all true and I think, looking back, that what was about to happen next may have saved my life yet again.

It was also wintertime and freezing cold with no heating in the house at all. I fell out of bed and having no way of getting back as I was too frail with wasted muscle to even move, let alone stand up. All I could remember was drifting in and out of consciousness, and I still have memories that I was absolutely fucking freezing. 1 can remember my whole life passing through my head, "Is this the end to this terrible illness which the alcohol was no longer helping me with?" The thought of death became more and more the best solution, a blessed end to drift away into unconsciousness and never resurface seemed to me the best way. I did not want to live anymore and yet for some reason I seemed to game the will, or was it the terrible intense cold that made me have a clarity of mind to move.

I could not stand. I remember shouting and screaming for help between periods of semi consciousness and blurring delusions. My wife did not come to me, but by chance a neighbour heard my cries for help. Unbeknown to me, she had tried without success to get into the house. Apparently she called the police. They broke the door down. The paramedics rushed me to hospital and I was in a terrible state, a disgusting state yet again. Total emaciation. I was this time totally fucked. My whole body was in a complete minimal state. How a man of previous great stature and mental competence could let his mind's addiction let him become such a mess, such a pitiful incapable diminished state God only knows. And yet my liver was ok, luckily with only slight damage.

I am not going to bore you again with all that happened to me in hospital during this stay. I have said it all before. Writing this book at this time in question, brings back to me so much total anguish, and it is impossible for me to open those memories and to put it into words, please forgive me.

But, the better I got yet again as I persevered and eventually managed to improve enough to get back home after a few months in hospital. I had by now spent more than 5 months in hospital. What a fucking waste of life, or did I want a life without the booze? I used to hear people say the most fucking stupid things like, "Why don't you drink alcohol free booze?" As if in their fucking stupid brains they thought you liked the fucking taste. What a lot of amazingly brainless fucking people there were out there. People in general could not understand or comprehend this terrible illness at all. **This ignorance of the terrible way of addiction really fucks me off big time.**

However, now I was home again something in my life was about to change forever. At least I could have a fag if nothing else. I had a lot of help from close friends wishing me well, but it can all mean nothing at all to you as instilled in yourself is that you have lost your only friend, the LIQUID ONE, and all you can really think of is that friend. In a way it's a bit like bereavement, constantly feeling the sad loss of a friend or even a loving pet. The only difference is that you are very tempted to regain your friend in the bottle, as this is so easy. Thoughts of, "I can cut down" or "drink weak beer" or whatever CAN start fucking your head.

All this is quite normal as a part of denial of the booze to your body; that your brain keeps trying to persuade you to succumb to its desire for alcohol is astounding. The power of the mind to put you, the host of your mind, back into destruction, a SELF-destruction, was overpowering and constant..

Maybe like me, you may agree to self-destruction, as I could see by now no life without the booze either. The following words were instilled in my head by my own mind.:

"I cannot live without the BOOZE and also I cannot live with it. Yes! You're fucked if you do and you are fucked if you don't. Either way you are fucked!"

I walked aimlessly around indoors. I was going out for long walks to try to keep my mind off the BOOZE, but for me and probably for you, it's a daily losing battle. Slowly, but surely, as the hours go by it can even make it worse. Depression sets in more with the hour by hour of constant thoughts of, "I must stop thinking of that booze; let's do something to take away my thoughts of booze." And depression was only ever solved by the friendly drink.

All I know is that it is like a ball going down a hill; the further it goes down the hill, the faster it goes. The more you think, "I must not drink," the more you seem to feel you **have** to have a drink. It was in all of these awful times that I found it easy to think I could just say, "fuck this life," and even if I won the lottery of millions of pounds, it would make no fucking difference. You cannot buy your health and also you can't buy yourself out of the awful mess either.

What a lonely place to be, physically and mentally lonely by day and miserably and feeling completely lonely by night. When you wake up you do so wanting more BOOZE. You feel desperate for it. In the past it had proved to wash away the depressions and the loneliness. ***When will this terrible mental undermining of the real truth disappear? Can I take anymore?***

Let me tell others who do not understand how lucky they are not to be on this sinking ship of addiction. I would give all my possessions away to just not to be on this ship. The night also had its own moments of despair: a soaking wet bed from cold sweating was my normal occurrence, with absolutely fearsome dreams, and all too often waking up with panic attacks.

Is all this fucking suffering worth it? How come my friends are still drinking and enjoying themselves without any drinking problems? Why me? I felt insanely jealous and envious of them all. Why me? What was I going to do? This was it for me; I just did not want a life without booze; there was no let up from the devil in the bottle, I now realized; there was no way that I could continue without it ANY LONGER!

By now my mental health was in other ways in a complete disarray as well. I felt an absolute mess with very strong thoughts of suicide to boot. My so-called drinking pals were no longer at my side either - it was quite strange really. In all honesty, I could now clearly see they were not really true friends; they were only people who sustained their overall habits with each other in a common mental easement with a drink.
In my hour of need I had become a total outcast. In any case, you very rarely see a full-blown alcoholic like me in a pub any way. You are too ill to get there for a start, let alone looking like a smelly tramp. How would anyone serve you looking and smelling like that?.

By now, at this time there was nothing left in my life. My business gone, my wife gone, my friends gone and that was it really for me. So, yes, I could not last another day without the booze. I didn't even *want* another day without the booze. I am sure it is hard to understand by the outsider looking in, but it was and probably still is impossible to understand unless you have also been in, or been touched by this situation.

So having little money I was straight onto the strong, cheap cider. It did not matter what it was, as long as it got you there where you wanted to be. Free again from the depressions and the loneliness. Of course, it did not take many weeks of this continued drinking to again take its toll on my body. I looked like an old man, felt like an old man and again started to not bother with eating either, it all led to emaciation again. By now I had moved on from the cider. I was drinking 24 cans of Guinness and one bottle of brandy within every 24 hours, day and night. I was just wasting away in my own piss sodden bed. Again into complete degradation of body and mind.

Of course, the only way that I could get booze was to ring the off-license with my booze requirements, get the total and write a cheque for the amount. Then I would ring a taxi to take the cheque to them and bring the booze back to me. This was fine for a while but in the end the cab firm could see how ill I had become and refused any more trips for me. I was now in a no-win situation. No booze, no food - not that I could keep it down anyway, and it was at this time I was starting to collapse and vomit frequently. Heaven knows for how long this phase went on as I had lost all understanding of hours or even days. There is no recollection of day or night. It just did not matter. I was passing in and out of consciousness. All I knew on waking was that I need to instantly grab the first can I could get my hands on.

At this point my whole body was covered with sores. There were deep sores on my thighs, and my knees were so painfully grazed and with sore infections from crawling around on the floor most of the time. By now I could not even get to stand up or drag myself up to get into bed either. I had not seen anyone at all now for weeks. My brothers had given up on me and my family was nowhere to be seen. It was immensely frightening and even in this pissed up state even I began to realise that the final end was near. I was vaguely aware I could not continue like this, *but I felt there was no way stopping it now.*

I felt so ill that even the feeling of sanctuary, of any release by getting another can quickly down was not there. The time between drinks was getting ever closer together. *The fire in me was now in full blaze!*

I was by now running low on being able to keep getting booze and my one thought, my only coherent thought was of different ways that I could somehow get more of the stuff. It's quite strange that the fear of running low on booze was all I could think of It was now my life, my whole life was consisting of only getting a drink, a can, a bottle, anything.. I can remember thinking how I was going to ring a cab to get them to bring me more, when I realised through the haze of my mind that I could barely stand up to make the call. But it is quite amazing that the longer you are without your chosen addiction, my alcohol, the willpower of your perverse mind in you becomes stronger to get more of its craved substance. That's what seemed to happen to me. I did somehow, I really cannot fully remember how though those blurred memories manage to make a call. This was, unbeknown to me, the last cab that I would ever ring.

Yes, I managed to call a cab and somehow pulled myself up into a chair, waiting for the cab to arrive. I sat fixated by looking at the clock, watching each minute tick by, impatiently watching the ten minutes they had said tick by! I began to have feelings of panic. It was now 15 minutes. My whole body was shaking in total anxiety because of the late arrival of the cab. All sorts of things were going through my mind. Maybe the cab firm had heard about me using a cab to collect my booze and wouldn't come. I remember whispering over and over again "Please, please come soon." That was the fear of withdrawals. At times like these you might even kill for the relief of a drink.

I beg of you reading this book that if you are at a lesser stage in this terrible illness, for God's sake try to come off it, seek help before you reach such a moment of nothingness, of degradation, of such a pitiful lowness of life and spirit.. Take it from me, it is unbearable.

But. back to the cab. Yes, it did arrive and I staggered to the door to open it, but I did not have the strength to unlock it. "Are you stuck mate?" he asked.
"Yes," I said making out it was the door and not I. However, with his help we
managed to open the door. His face was aghast when he looked at me. "What the fuck have you been up to? You look like you have done ten rounds with
Mike Tyson!" my face was covered in carpet bums from using my face to push
myself up from the floor sometimes when I collapsed. My knees and arms looked the
same. Of course, smelling like a polecat did not go down well either.
"Where do you want to go?" he asked.

25

"To the nearest off-license, any shop that sells booze." I replied. He reluctantly started the cab and off we went.

On getting to the off-license there was no way of me having the strength to get the booze, so he ended up buying it for me. On the way back home all that was in my mind was to get booze down me to relieve withdrawals. It seemed to take forever. He started talking to me like 'you look awful, you need help mate' and I remember saying to him that I had just brought my help, that I was past all help.

"Now you listen to me mate," he replied, "take my card, and if you ever need anything, or need help, just ring." I just took the card and put it in my pocket. My whole mind and thoughts were on getting home. It was with relief that I actually fell out of the cab when he stopped at home. He picked me up and helped me down to my door and opened it for me with my key.

"Let's get you inside mate," he said. On entering my house the look on his face at the state of my place, was shattering. With the whole floor covered in cans and bottles, he asked me, "Look mate, you live on your own in this mess?"
"Yes," I replied. He was quite concerned leaving me on my own but I said. "Thanks for all you have done."
"Don't lose my card, will you," he replied, "Like I said, just ring if in need." He left after that. God only knows what I did with that card. All that was in my mind was getting my friend in the bottle down inside me so he could ease that terrible need..

But God only knew what the card would bring.

The booze that we brought home did not last long, only days, and then I was back in the same horrendous situation. I can remember looking up at the clock. It was about 5 o'clock in the morning and my body was craving more booze. However, there was no more, and the fear of the withdrawal was overwhelming. It did not even occur to me to think of the card as all my brain could think of was to get more booze. Like a fool I managed to get in my car with no concern for myself or anybody else on the road either. My mind only focused on the nearest shop! God only knows how I did not kill myself driving or run over any innocent bystanders. Sometimes I still cringe thinking of how stupid I was, but at the time only fear of having no booze, was my only concern. Anything, absolutely anything to stop the withdrawals.

I was driving around my local shops, but my search became fruitless as they were all closed, it was too early. I became more anxious, frantically anxious. There seemed no way I could get any alcohol. My only hope was to drive to my very close friend Trevor. "Trevor has always got drink in his house," was the only thing going through my head. I managed to get there and literally started bashing at the door with all my puny strength. If I could have, I'd have broken the door down. Obviously he was still in bed asleep, but eventually he heard me and opened the door, and I remember just falling through it. What a bloody state I was in, bursting into tears, shouting just to get me a drink. He helped me up from the floor and took me inside. At this point even he was crying in total disbelief of how I had become such an absolute physical and mental wreck.

At first he refused to give me a drink but in the end reluctantly gave in to my pleas. The first can of booze went straight down and I can recall just waiting with my head in my lap for the booze to take effect. Trevor was very deeply upset, and gave me a hug for some reassurance, or whatever was on his mind, I do not know.

It wasn't long before I was asking for another drink, but this time Trevor refused. "Just give me a fucking drink," I pleaded. I was at his mercy and too ill to do anything about it, except plead to him to give me my saviour, my friend who could cure all these horrible feelings and depressions. Again he refused. He only said: "What are we going to do with you?" I think that at that moment I realized that there was no way forward for me, I was on the bottom step of the ladder with no will to carry on living. These words cannot ever explain the situation I was now in: The desperation. The realisation again that I CANNOT LIVE WITH IT, AND CANNOT LIVE WITHOUT IT.

It again made me understand through my pain that death would be the only way out of this living hell, however self indulgent and stupid that might sound. It was the only idea to give me any relief that seemed left to me. Trevor and I talked together and cried together and of course, apart from feeling seriously ill, there was immense guilt in me that my illness was seriously affecting other close people who were having their lives ruined by me.

I think it was me that suggested that somehow Trevor would get me home and stay with me. It was as if we both knew that my life would otherwise be coming to an end. It was devastating to see the immense anguish on his face. God only knew what was going on in his head. I dreaded the thought. My family was not in this scenario at all and there was no point in trying to contact them either. They had given up on me and it was, I suppose, less upsetting for them and I could understand it.

However, we managed to get back to my home, my pigsty, my beautiful home turned into nothing more than an Alco's den, awash with cans and bottles piss and shit. In fact, it was hell for him to get me to my chair, and even then all I could do or even think about was trying to tip the dregs out of all the empty cans into my beer mug.

In retrospect I realise now what a fucking terrible and disgusting state to be in!

I can recall Trevor saying that he was going to call the ambulance. Call them he did but was informed that they would not come to my house anymore. Even they had now given up on me! Trevor also rang Social Services about me. Again the same result: "We can do no more for Alan," Trevor was told. We both broke down crying and hugging each other and started talking about all the good times and all the things we had achieved together in our working lives over 30 years.

To some degree in me there was a form of relief that this living hell was drawing to a close. The booze had beaten me; the earlier saviour had turned into the devil itself; my friend in the bottle had also deceived me. Please, please believe me that it's worse than being on death row.

I pleaded with Trevor to get me on top of my disgusting bed and to just lie with me and cuddle me, talk to me and not to let go of me. The unmanageable, rising fear in me was horrendous. We both eventually must have fallen asleep. Time was of no importance at this stage; there was no importance any more. Upon waking up some time later, Trevor got me off the bed and put me back in my chair, *and that was the start of the beginning of the end or the end of the beginning.*

There was no booze in the house and that awful fear of no friend in my glass was devastating, and I cannot describe how ill I felt either. It was a living hell with nowhere to go. In my head Trevor was my saviour, he will go and get me some more booze. On pleading with him he refused, saying that I would be dead in a week. "I cannot be a part of that. I cannot do it, do you understand?" he said bursting into tears as well. It was bloody awful to see people around me also totally devastated by this illness of mine, and themselves feeling totally useless as they could do no more for me.

I was fiddling with a card that was just amongst all the other rubbish on the coffee table and on it was a phone number. It was the card that the taxi driver had given me.
I remember his last words to me, "If you need help or anything, just ring me". I told Trevor what the taxi driver had said to me.
"What have we got to lose," Trevor replied. "There is no-one else". There was an immense calm that seemed to enter the room. You could feel it. A feeling of hope; a feeling of love; very difficult to describe; a very strong feeling that both of us have never encountered before in our lives. It was amazing!

I could hear in my head the words "you are not going to drink anymore, you are not going to die". Was I going mad? No, I could hear it; I could feel it; it was very real. Both of us were witnessing this very strange loving force. If I had experienced this on my own the pundits could have said: "You didn't even know what day it was and you expect us to believe that?"

But it was true, and at that precise moment my life was about to change. There was an urgency to ring the number on the card. After telling the man who I was and my situation, he remembered me. I told him that my situation had worsened since we last met. To my amazement he said that he would drop everything and come and be with me within 20 minutes. All this seemed as if it was meant to be and a calm was very present in the house. You could feel its presence. Of course at this time there was no way of me understanding any of this. Nobody would.

The taxi driver was true to his word. He knocked on the door and Trevor let him in. I will never forget the utter sadness on his face as he entered the room, walking on all the cans and bottles that covered the floor to be by my side. He was looking at me in disbelief of how a very fit, professional person could have gotten to this state of health. My face was scarred with carpet bums and sores all over my body and totally emaciated with not the strength to even lift a cigarette to my own lips. I can remember him holding my hand and saying a prayer, praying to God for help. Again there was that feeling of peace and tranquillity that was adorning the room. Unbeknown to me at this time, it was the Holy Spirit, the Spirit of God Himself, which became more apparent over the following months.

If you are NOT a believer in God, I beg of you not to put this book down at this moment. Please give me a chance to help you, to help yourself. There is a hope, also a chance for you, so please read on to understand this very time and compelling story before making a judgment. I was in no fit state at this time to understand or even think of anything either. God was not in my head at all; nothing was in my head; only a strong feeling of peace and a new will to survive.

It turned out that the taxi driver's name was Paul. It was the first time I heard his name and this name would be instilled in me forever. It was first decided for them to get me into the bath as I smelt terrible and I had not had a change of clothing for weeks on end and even I was surprised at the state of my naked body. It was covered with sores and my bones stuck out. What a bloody state of a human being I had become, terrible and by my own hand, disgusting! But bath me they did and got me back into bed.

Paul explained to me that he would stay with me at all times. Was I hearing him right?

"Put your trust in me, I will not let you down," he said.
It seemed impossible that at last there was one person who would look after me. He suggested that food was the most important thing first. Scrambled eggs seemed like a good idea, but of course I could not even lift a spoon to my mouth. Paul started to feed me but it was not easy to keep food down at all. It made me retch. We decided to have a little at a time and often, and in that way it was not so bad. Now drifting in and out of sleep, it was such a comfort to have and clean, warm bed and someone laying beside me, another human being giving a feeling of security and caring.. I was filled with a feeling of peaceful warmth inside me.

Over the next few days my intake of food increased without anymore retching. So on this front, things were improving although I was still bedridden and skeletal. However, the previously constant feeling of my need for the booze was now no longer filling my mind. The intense withdrawals that I had encountered when taken to hospital before were no longer there. I felt tentative relief. It all seemed too good to be true, as if this was supposed to be, having Paul looking after me 24 hours a day, seven days a week. It was in itself unbelievable, a chance in a million to have a complete stranger give up his job to stay with me. You work it out. Looking back for me this was truly a gift from God.

As the weeks passed, there was a great improvement in me, now I was standing and walking under my own steam, and I could feel in me there was now, at last a way forward, free from what I was now able to see as the living hell. I even felt inspired to go forward and start living again. Paul thought that we should now go to an AA (Alcoholics Anonymous) meeting and see if that would help me further. Having not been to a meeting before, I was amazed on arrival at the meeting, the level of friendship there was, and to witness all types of people from surgeons to dustmen.

I heard how the addiction to booze had totally wrecked their lives. It was as if all that were there sitting in the group, could relate with each other. I cannot praise the AA movement enough for what they stand for. They are entirely funded by themselves, with no political view or any particular religion. The doors were open to all. I recommend this to anyone to go and experience the A A for what it really is. At my first visit to the AA the group was in deep discussion how some of them had been saved from death by what the AA call the Higher Power. This higher Power stepped in at the last moment in their lives and of course this higher Power they are relating to is God. I am not here to try to change their description of the God Almighty as their higher Power, as we are all individuals to which we are all entitled to our own views. So I do fully understand not to upset anybody unnecessarily that there is probably no better name than the HIGHER POWER.

But let's move on to those who were at the meeting describing how in the last stages of addiction, like myself with no hope and death looming, they also encountered a spiritual happening.

I cannot tell you how good it was to be around people who had had the same experiences, as if we were all one with the same true story to tell. The Holy Spirit saving them in their darkest hour, like myself. Questions were raised during this very emotional debate. Why did God step into our lives and not others? For my own belief the answer to this question is that God only knows. Perhaps this is where the saying 'God only knows' comes from and who are we to question the reasoning of the God Almighty. In my case a whole new life for me was beginning to come true. Why is it that very famous people from singers, actors and footballers' who are household names to many, could not give up the BOOZE, even with the Media encouraging them to stop and also having the means to afford Private Dry Out Clinics. I do believe that no one on the planet knows.

In the discussion at the AA there were four people basically the same as myself and it came to me how many other people throughout the world were in this spiritual healing position of hope and cure that they had not brought upon themselves. This was the work of the Higher Power. Unless it happens to yourself and I sincerely hope that it does, welcome it with loving arms as I did, even though at the time this love, this inner feeling of hope was still very confusing for me. However, I knew that I was not on my own in this hellhole of booze and there was a light at the end of the tunnel. Although it was still small, I had a growing faith - a faith that later on became my absolute saviour to move on to a glittering new life.

The weeks were flying past and every day there were more improvements in my health and mental state. Paul was my saviour. In all this time looking back, he was also meant to be in this whole scenario. Yes, it takes some believing, but it is true. But still this was only the start of the beginning for me. Paul was a Christian and always invited me to go to church with him but I always declined. I had so much to catch up on in my life and around the farm, which had become in disarray during my illness. However, something told me it was not yet the right time to go to the church. I could not understand this although there was a feeling I had to wait, stay where I was. A mixture of feelings, very difficult to describe, were whirling inside me, but there was contentment in me that I had never felt before in my whole life.

Paul had moved to the farm, living in the mobile home and was always on hand to give me help in all ways. I was very glad to have him around me, always seeming to give me hope for the future. My wife decided to leave me - the woman who had been by my side for so much of my life, gone. It felt like a bereavement in some way, as we had been friends all through our school going years, going out with each other at sixteen and later getting married. We had two lovely daughters from our marriage of 35 years. Why would my lovely wife throw all this away at a time in our lives when we had just seen a way forward without the booze in both of us?

I was now busy with divorce procedures and trying to cope with all the stress and worry that comes with it. Many people thought that I would, in my now very unpleasant stressful state of mind would yet again succumb to the booze. Strangely, it seemed to have the opposite effect on me. The more grief that came my way only enhanced my inner feelings of a future without the booze. I could sense it, feel it, there was some loving presence at my side at all times.

Even more sadness was on its way. Paul, my soul mate through all this, was diagnosed with cancer. I cannot tell you how bad this affected me. The man that I honestly believe was sent to me to be my saviour, was now dying himself The following months were very hard to swallow and to this day it still brings tears to my eyes. We would talk or laugh or cry together and I could not understand why he was ill. It felt like a dream, but it was becoming a very real one, and it had a deep emotional effect on me

I started to question his religious faith; a faith which seemed to have let him down. But all he would say was that God sometimes worked in what appeared to be strange ways to us. Again with all this sadness in me, booze was not in my head. Far from it! I think Paul must have realised in his mind that maybe that I would not be able to take the end result. To my horror, one morning, his car had gone and he had left the farm. This absolutely broke my heart at that time, in that moment. On reflection, however, I now understand that it would have been impossible to say goodbye to him in his last hours.

I was desolate. What more was this fucking life going to throw at me? You must understand. Even ask yourself: " Do you think you would still have stayed
off the booze?" Only you know the answer to that one.

However, all was not lost, as some days later I went into his mobile home and on the table was a letter to me. This would turn my life full circle.

The letter was words

from the Bible

Jeremiah 29:11:14

for I know the plans I have for you declares
The Lord, plans to prosper you and not to
harm you. Plans to give you hope and a
future;
then you will call upon me and come and pray to me and I will listen to
you. you will seek me and find me.
When you seek me with all your heart, I will be found by you.
declares The Lord, and will bring you back from captivity.
I will gather you from all the nations and places where I have banished
you,
declares The Lord, and will bring you back to the place from which I
carried you into
exile.

At the bottom of the letter it just carried on to say
(PS. Go the best is yet to come, Alan)

All of these beautiful words at this time did not as I see it looking back mean much else than just lovely words to me I suppose, but there was a mix of confusion in my mind, why did Paul leave this part of the Bible, what does it mean to me, in fact did not relate to me at all as far as I can see, and off-course the P.S. seamed all so far away, I kept the note as it meant a lot to me.

However, the months were racing by and my strength was returning, and I had not had a drink for now over a year, it was a lonely place however now on my own, lost my wife, lost Paul, and where were my close friends gone still in the pub, it's amazing how when you don't drink you do not fit in with them anymore to some degree, sometimes it was also apparent that they actually felt embarrassed to come to my house as if I may be tempted to go up the pub with them or it was said by some that they also felt guilty to drink in my presence. To me all this was utter rubbish as the booze was in no way in my head and in fact I often went to the pub for lunch and not bothered at all by the smell or the long, long gone urge to get some drown, it was now becoming a total relief to have also lost my friend in the bottle, but I was about to make a new one.

The Calling

Yes the calling is the only word that I can describe the next chapter in my life, a call that completely changed me, my outlook and my inner self in one wonderful moment.

It was just an ordinarily Saturday evening to me, I was watching the TV, but then there seemed to be a stillness in the room, very calming, a feeling of inner love and contentment came within me and I could hear a voice in my head - am I going mad? No this was very real. It was in me, it filled my mind. All I could hear was "In the morning Alan you are going to church", and that was all. A single statement with conviction. The words I heard, but additionally, there was an absolute peace within me, although I was still feeling slightly confused all at the same time.

On awaking on the Sunday morning the presence, the calmness and conviction was still there. It steered me to wash and dress properly in a suit .To get Suited and Booted and that's what I did. I was asking myself, in my head, "what am I doing?" and replying to myself "you're going to church."

As I got in the car and drove off, I was asking myself "where am I going, to which church?" But to my amazement at the cross road there was a definite voice saying, turn left and go up to St. Andrews church and that I did. Parking the car at the church somehow felt quite normal, and not new to me at all, as if I had done this many times before.

Now entering the door of the church I stood still for a moment, taking everything in, my eyes scanning the people, the walls and ceiling, and at that moment **I knew by being in God's house that I was also home.** A feeling at long last of love and inner self peace, and with a future, *and* all sorts of other new feelings were now all flowing in me, brought about in me by the Holy Spirit.

As the weeks went by going to church every Sunday, my whole life was now entirely on a new path. It meant, for me, making new friends going on to even joining the adult choir and all these things gave me a completely new outlook on life as if it was pre-destined and meant to be. My life was starting again without my friend in the bottle and it was so much better than I could ever have imagined. **The Lord had found me and, greater still, I had found the Lord.**

After the Calling

Now, with a much clearer head, my very unfortunate past seemed like a very bad dream. But a nightmare that somehow had a good ending. Off-course, now I was starting to put the whole picture together. From the gaining of my end at deaths door, the Holy Spirit even God himself stepped in to save me. Why me? I know that this will become very apparent in the years to come. Even I will have to wait for God's reason. Looking back over all this biography, let me ask you the following questions: what were the chances of me finding the piece of card with the taxi drivers phone number, and what complete stranger would do all that Paul did - from feeding me, staying with me and giving up his job to help me to recover to the person that 1 am today?. It is from the Lord himself

Now let's look back to the words in the letter that Paul left for me on the table. *For I know the plans I have for you declares the Lord. Plans to prosper you and not harm you. Plans to give you a hope and a future.*

Even the first 3 lines mean so much. I know the Lord has plans for me. I know that now I'm prospering. I know that now I have hope and I have a future.

Yes powerful words but they are so true to me and in me and can be in you also. The love of God is all around us. Let Him come into your life like he came into mine, and let yourself find Him.

The following lines are so true *{Then you will call upon me).* Yes I went to church, this first day.

(Pray *to me and I will listen to you)*
Yes I prayed and all came true to me

(You will seek, me and find me).
Yes even going through the church door for the first time, I was home. I had found God.

{When you seek me with all your heart, I will be found by you, declares The Lord).
Yes this is also so true. I found the Lord with all my heart and it feels so lovely, and knowing that the Lord is at my side to help me through the day, to show me the way, in times of despair, and all the rest of the words are very true to me.

But off-course I now also know why Paul
left the words. *{PS. **The best is yet to come**)*

How true these words have became to me. Now I know the meaning of life in those words, the immense new hope, the new friends, and a whole new life which is emerging, the new love in me towards others. I now have an inner contentment in myself. All this is from the Lord himself.

There can be no one on this planet that can dispute these words as they are the words of the God Almighty and I can only pray that if at this present time you are in the hands of the devil in the bottle that your prayers for help will be answered.

As I see it, there are only 2 people left that are now in your life to help you, one is yourself with God's help, the other at this time is me. So do not give up no matter how ill you feel, or how close at deaths door or even how lost you feel. Everything, including yourself and your life can change and become new and exciting. I am living proof that with faith there is a way forward to a new life, a new life with the God Almighty. Let the Holy Spirit enter in and feel the love that it brings. Jesus gave his own life for us, let's not ever forget it. The Romans lived to regret the **crucifixion,** even in their own words of their history they realised that they had killed the true Son of God.

The love of alcohol is an addiction. It is the devil in the bottle that, despite yourself, can and will destroy you.

Give yourself into the power and love of The true Messiah, Jesus Christ.

Of course there is as always the opposite of Christ's powers and love and that is the devil himself, who is always looking around like a vulture to take any opportunity to enter your body for his own gain, the devil will always enter, when you are at a low ebb, and will make your life a complete misery whether its financial, health, marriage breakdowns, - the list is endless.

There is no doubt at all that if you let the Holy Spirit into your life there is only one way the devil can go and that is to leave, and always remember that by having the love of God in you and having faith, no Christian is afraid of the devil. The devil is afraid of you.

I sincerely hope that you have found this first part of the book moving and sincerely hope that to whatever stage of this terrible illness you are in you can have a way forward that you may feel to be at the present time totally out of your reach. Your problems are really in your mind. Your mind is strong and guides you, but can be perverted by the devil, and to fight this can be difficult on your own. But, your mind can be changed. Always keep an open mind to allow the Holy Spirit to enter into your life and I pray that the God Almighty will hear your prayers and change your life forever, as He did mine and to that there can be no greater gift that the Lord can give you, a new positive life with inner peace and love, even an eternal life in His love.

The number of people, uncountable numbers, that have died an agonising and degrading death of this terrible illness of addiction is tragic, we can only pray that they are now at peace in death. But, it can be changed. There is a way back to a proper life. A way back to a life of positive love and peace.

Believe me there is a living peace and a whole new future.

There are only 2 options left to you - if you are really honest with yourself Yes its hard, and also you may or not be a Christian, It doesn't matter. Either way God is always by our side, if you seek the Lord with all your heart and let the love of Christ and the Holy Spirit enter your body, you will have a new life without the booze, without the addiction which will drag you down. You can rise out of that degradation forever, with a new freedom from the hell in the bottle.

Footprints

These are very powerful and

meaningful words: ***One night a***

man had a dream,
he dreamed he was walking along the beach with The Lord.
Across the sky flashed scenes from his life, and in
each scene he noticed two sets of foot prints in the sand,
one belonging to him and the other to The Lord.
When the last scene of his life flashed before him
he looked back at the footprints in the sand
he noticed that many times along the path of his life
there was only one set of footprints
he also noticed that it happened at the very lowest
and saddest times in his life.
That really bothered him and he questioned The Lord about it
Lord you said that once I decided to follow you
you'd walk with me all the way
but I have noticed that during the most troublesome
times in my life, there is only one set of
footprints. I don't understand why when I needed you most you would leave me The Lord replied "My precious, precious child I love you and I would never leave you.
During your times of trial
and suffering when you see
only one set of footprints it
was then that I carried
you??

author unknown

In my times when I might feel low these loving words in Footprints always brings home to me that I am never really on my own. He is there if I need Him.

40

Above all stick to the task of overcoming the power, the alcoholic addictive poison in the bottle, and also keep the following words at hand in times of despair:

LORD,
help me to remember that nothing is going to happen to me today that you and I can't handle together

Pray to the Lord those words and He will hear you, and always will be by your side to help and comfort you, in your darkest hour.

Coining to Terms

As I said in the introduction of this book that I will hopefully become your saviour, as there can be no living person on this planet that understands what you are going through more than me, and in the following pages we can, together find that there is an answer to your personal addiction.

However, the road ahead will not be easy there is no easy way, but day by day it will become better and better. Never look back, look forward with only a positive need for freedom of this hellish illness of addiction, whether alcohol, or any other poison taken into our system that perverts our mind into driving us to degradation and ultimate death by the Devil. That nearly no one can comprehend unless you have been there, or are there right now.

There are many stages of alcoholism, we are all different, with varying amounts of resistance to alcohol that each person must or may consume, only you know in what stage you are in, some people having a social drink after work see that as no problem and nor do I for that matter, but for others that may also not be the case, only you know and in the following page try to establish to what degree of addiction you are in as a individual.

The fact is that as a nation, we are probably the world's worst. The UK has a history of drink and drug abuse and let's face it, what can be more relaxing and socially acceptable than the British pub a social, friendly drink?.

There are many categories to which you may fall into from the 'A a pint of bitter men to the two bottles of Scotch man or the glass of wine lady to the 3 bottles of wine a day lady.

First of all why do you drink? Be honest with yourself if you can.

Is it because you just enjoy it, the social side, meeting friends, having a laugh, or is it the booze comes first then all of the above comes second? (I wonder). Or is your life in such a mess that you need to get out of reality or depression for a few hours, or even worse you are already totally alcohol dependent?.

All drinkers use any excuse to themselves to justify a piss up from wetting the baby's head to the funeral wake, from getting married or divorce, to being broke or winning a lottery? We use all types of excuses to justify over drinking habits. But when does our habit become dependency?

Every person that drinks daily is, whether you like it or not an alcohol dependent. Alcohol dependency is not being an alcoholic and if you are alcohol dependent and not a full-blown alcoholic there are many ways to stop.

Now this is the question that you must ask yourself if you realise you are alcohol dependent: if I carry on the way I am there is a chance that my present drinking will remain at the same level? If you feel you can honestly say to yourself, yes. Good. And, it could well do, but it could, and usually does in most people, over a period, maybe over a few years, gradually get worse, and everything around you will slowly disintegrate and you will lower into degradation to afford the alcoholic intake to keep your addiction in your mind satisfied..

So in this chapter *Coming to terms* it is so important to do just that. However hard that might seem at the time. Remember, the alcohol twists your mind to joke about your drinking, to justify it. But, if you would find it too difficult to resist a drink for more than a couple of days, you are alcohol dependent.

My Friends

Your friends in the pub are mainly only that really, and no more than that. Its only because you are all in the same boat that on the surface they appear to be friends. A happy, jokey mood and light banter, perhaps. But they are only drinking friends and take it from me, in most cases when you give up the booze and maybe drink soft drinks in their company, it then becomes apparent that you are no longer in the fold. Most people who are inebriated and pissed cannot relate to a sober person in their group. Even worse still is to be sober and listen to a group of pissed up people, who sound stupid and behave in a ridiculous way. To them clever and finny, but to you stupid and worse than childish. So you will find that you slowly drift away from that environment and social group of losers. You will find that you will not even bother to even go to the pub at all. You will make new friends, real friends over time. This seems almost impossible in the early stages of being away from your drinking friends, but you will find greater depths of friendship..

It is a common effect of addiction that some will, perhaps sub-consciously, actually feel guilty in drinking, and they will try to justify their addiction by sharing it with you. They themselves will try to tempt you and influence you into giving in and start drinking again. It's an old saying, birds of a feather stick together. But who, in all honesty wants to be in that group of birds?

There is a way forward in all this, and it will soon become apparent that the phone calls asking if you are going up the boozer tonight or whatever invitation to indulge in the addiction or whatever will slowly stop. Yes it probably sounds awful but it is the truth, and so say to yourself "well done" Really, if you think about it you are now probably somewhat pissed off by being their sober taxi driver as well if the truth be known?

I know it's not easy. I used to sit in the pub with my pint of orange juice with the hope to find some sort of comfort but as it was not there it will never be there not in the way it used to be and in the early stages you are clinging on to a way of habit and that's all it is. Habit! To some of-course the pub is an absolute no go area after giving up the booze, so loneliness may set in on the friends front but your life will change with new friends, and forget about your drinking friends, and your old evil best friend in the bottle.

So let me also tell you that none of my drinking pals ever visited me in hospital or ever in any way helped me in my hours of need. That's all they are in most cases only drinking pals. Propping up the bar often stupidly thinking they are putting the world to right.
It will not be easy for you to forget the past, for you cannot change it, but you can readjust your view of it. You can change the future with new friends, real friends that maybe always wanted to be your friend really, but kept their distance because you seemed to have a pub social life. They may be steered away from you because of your drinking in some cases.

Coming to Terms with Myself - When to Give-up?

When is the time to give-up, yes its somewhat like putting off the dentists appointment, in reality if you do this that day will never come, or you may blame all sorts of financial problems, family and work pressure the list is endless and even if there are no reason to add to this list, you will only invent any excuse in your mind to justify another drink or piss up, you know this is true, be absolutely honest with yourself, in fact you are being torn at this moment, you want to give up but your body does not, the brain is craving for more.

This craving can be mild or be so intense that you would do anything for another drink, even beg, steal or borrow, there are many rungs on the ladder from the desperate bottom to the top, either way you must come to terms, however hard the road becomes, or seems, to be honest there is no time, this is going to be better than any other time, the time is now, the time for a future and happiness, or if, you are on the bottom of the ladder there is no time left, hard but that's it, yes you do not really want to hear this do you? I'm sure inside you say *no,* but please keep reading on for your own salvation. There were many times in my own self when I desperately tried to give up and I do really understand the hellish anguish you are in, but do not make the big mistake that I did before my salvation by the Lord himself, why did I put myself through hell with withdrawals on numerous occasion, over and over again.
Always thinking the need for a drink was to welcome in an old, comforting friend ....
as it continued to ease me into death.
Learn by my stupid mistakes, only give-up once, hold on, however difficult, and persevere and make this effort to break the grip of alcoholic poisoning. Break the addiction. Break the addiction NOW.

Coming to Terms - What sort of

Drinker are you? The Social Drinker

Most people that I would call social drinkers are nothing more serious than just that. They can either take it or leave it, and the drinking in its self is not of any great importance, some only drink because everyone else in the group of friends is doing so and having a glass in your hand is also more comforting something to fiddle with etcetera, and the feeling of getting pissed or even merry to some is a no go situation. They, luckily may be afraid of getting pissed, of losing control, or disgracing themselves. They can treat alcohol as something to have from time to time.

No one really knows why some of us can control alcohol to this degree all of their lives and why some cannot. I can remember one man at an AA meeting that had not ever drank in his life before and he explained that on having his first pint of larger he was instantly hooked and carried on to become a full blown alcoholic and had lost everything in his life, strange how one person can vary from one to another but off-course if we were all the same wouldn't life be boring, how great it must be to carry on drinking all your life if you are lucky enough to be just a social drinker, and really if you feel that you are just that, a social drinker then really enjoy it and carry on in that controlled way, but always be aware. If it becomes more than an occasional drink. If it becomes a regular event for whatever reason, that very slowly it can make you become a *regular* drinker that goes to the pub for a drink not like the social drinker that goes to an event where the drink is secondary to where you are.

If ever you feel that the events are becoming a way of justifying a drink then you are to some degree bordering to the line of being a *regular drinker,* take heed and enjoy drink for what it is not what it can become, an addiction that can ruin you, your life and all your relationships with those you hold dear..

Coming to Terms - the Regular Drinker

Yes the *regular drinker* falls into many formats whether going to the pub every dinnertime or evening or maybe regularly drinking at home, anybody that does this is without doubt an *alcohol dependent* to varying degrees, it's quite strange that the understanding philosophy of most people is to accept this as a way of a reasonable lifestyle, and it seems socially acceptable to do this even, non-drinkers saying what a great person he or she is. But, the fact is they are already becoming an addict with a love of an alcoholic drink. It is a stage of alcoholism. To most of these alcoholic dependent people it seems to be a reasonable and even great or exciting and friendly sociable thing to do, without any thought of the ultimate consequences of the future, the ill-health that it brings and terrible upset and possible destruction to the love of family life as well.

The *regular* and *alcoholic dependent* drinker will always have drink in their minds even at work looking forward to the first pint or straight down the pub at weekends and evenings. Unbeknown to all *regular* and *alcoholic dependent* drinkers the booze is becoming the first thing in their lives, as they begin using various excuses (which seem reasonable to them) for a drink.

To many people it is a way of relief to take the strain of the day away or a sort of reward for ones hard day at work, whatever the reason, they are still only excuses for the addict of the booze.

If you feel by reading the above that I am being offensive in anyway, that you are unharmed in the level of addiction described, and unfortunately you are in a difficult place. Please stop and think. Clear your mind of the overpowering addiction.

If you do not want to face a life without a drink, it is not an easy path to change and break away. To many they can see no way of life without alcohol, the socially acceptable drink, or see no harm in it for themselves, you are already deluding yourself And, of-course others around you maybe already be seriously suffering as their help or support is used to continue on your path, as the power of the booze starts overwhelming any positive thoughts that may enter your head, *any addict always puts the addiction first, most times not even realising that they are doing so..*

Drinking at home has become more in vogue in recent times due to drink / driving problems getting to and from the boozer and also the cost of drinking in the pub or the need to smoke whilst drinking. It's so easy now and so cheap to buy from the supermarket and also if you are a smoker why do you want to have a smoke outside a pub maybe in the rain and in the winter when you can do both in your own home, or a suitable shelter, a hole, a place to somehow exist. To some degree cheap booze and the smoking ban has opened up a can of worms for the regular alcohol drinker, and without any doubt the cause of many people's total addiction to increase without any restriction. Having drink at home can be absolutely fatal to many, and the comfort of the home can mask the addition which can very steadily creep up on you, until you may not even be able to keep living in your own home any more..

It is so easy to drift easily into starting to drink earlier and earlier in the day. Until the somehow justified craving has no time limits, no allocated time, just a need whenever you can get alcohol into yourself

If any of this is *you* then take it from me the future will become ever more evil that most of you cannot and will not be able handle it until it is far too late, until the final end in disgusting, degraded and terrible death.

I even dread the thought of you in such a condition..

Being just a regular drinker is only the tip of the iceberg, you are probably already alcoholically dependent. You may still have time to be just ease back to being just an occasional drinker, and not slide, without noticing, into being a full-blown alcoholic. The choice is yours NOW.

Coming to Terms - the Binge Drinker

The person that can go without the booze for maybe a week, a month or whatever time, then for some reason, not always a stressful reason, or for no reason at all goes on a bender to a degree of even near fatal alcohol poisoning is devastating to many that live their lives otherwise normally. The sudden, often only partly realised bang as the need to go on a the binge takes hold, to some people it may only last a night or a day, perhaps with friends. or alone, can be a symptom even more dangerous.

There was a person that I was in hospital with who apparently only had the immense urge maybe every 6 months. Not, you would think an addiction. Every time this occurred the only way of stopping him drinking was to be actually hospitalised. Binge drinking is highly dangerous and every binge drinker knows how lonely this terrible existence can be, even when hinging with so called friends, but often without friends and relatives even knowing that they have what might be thought a real drink problem at all.

All I can say to any binge drinker that my heart goes out to you. Your situation will probably get easier.
Let's look forward together further on in the book and I hope give you a salvation from this terrible situation - for all situations of the regular drinking of alcohol is an addiction. A terrible and destructive addiction..

Coming to Terms - the Top-up Drinker to a Serious Problem

For some people in this top-up alcoholic situation is can be a complete nightmare depending on what level your top-up level is, so let's start with the sort of person that is already a regular drinker, some will have a session in the pub, just a pint or three perhaps, then come home for example, and that is the end of their drinking until the next day or week depending on their habit. However, the top-up drinker usually to others never seems to get pissed or drunk at all, but without others realising requires a regular intake of alcohol throughout the session, day or night. Some will leave a drinking session to go home and after a short stay indoors will go back out again to drink elsewhere - or perhaps stay at home and have new drinks there. There is really no let-up if you are in this very unfortunate position. There is also a type of thrill if you like that so that every time you start drinking yet again it seems as if it's your first drink again - with a very pleasing state of mind or again a total relaxing feeling - that uncontrollable urge to recreate the feeling of that first drink.

I once knew a man that would always say time to go home or I will not be able to come out again. So then you go out if you are like this, and you are not alone either. But of course to some who drink indoors it can be a constant bottle even hiding the booze away to exaggerate the finding of it again, an odd, even perverse excitement if you like ...but, in fact just another top-up. Another feeding of the addiction that is going to take you ever further down.

The top-up drinker is in a hell-hole really, with him- or herself bordering on being a full blown alkie. A full blown addict. A full blown slide to oblivion, destruction and degradation, ignominy and to death.

To friends, neighbours or even family it is possible to be not aware of quite how your constant your level of alcoholic intake is, or to what level of addiction you have sunk into. Your actual state is probably deliberately hidden from them as much as you can. This sometimes becomes a sort of private addiction to some, keeping up appearances with a tidy house, maybe a well kept garden tidy dress etc. These are all to disguise the constant and slowly increasing dependency of the addiction. Trying to keep it your secret. You and your friendly alcohol. Even going to work and drinking in the toilets or a cupboard, wherever, with no one knowing what a state you are already in, but rest assured your addiction and your health will suffer increasingly in the short or long-term.

There are also many people that take a drink in their pocket or handbag when they go out with friends to drink in-between rounds because they cannot wait for the next person to finish theirs; then go to the toilet to get some more down in-between rounds and so on. Anything to try and get into that state of ease with your alcohol friend.

If you are in this top-up drink situation you will find that over a period of time the gap between one drink and another well decrease and may even wake you in the night as well with awesome feelings. Most people in this horrible state of addiction start to also put food last or maybe not eat much at all, if this is the case you are really only a whisker of being nearly full blown alcoholic

The longer this goes on the lower you will become, your occupation could be on the line, or you may already lost your job or wrecked your career.

It's a very frightening place to find you have no money for booze. I know I've been there, and the strange thing also is that if you had drinking palls, in most cases they will have dropped you like a stone; your family may have also finally given up and deserted you as well.

If you are any or more of the above I can only seriously sympathise in the desperate and terrible hell hole that you are now in, very few people can understand what level of ill feeling that you have inside. In my opinion you must at some point been there to even remotely understand how ill, really ill, desperate and incapable you feel inside. Knowing that another drink is the only partial relief you can have, to know that only one will only lead to another. To know, somewhere deep inside that you might never again reach that point where a drink, or perhaps any number of drinks will again achieve the friendliness of your friend alcohol. But, you know there is nothing else you want to do but try another drink. What a bloody mess you are now in, you know you are, but still the booze probably comes first. It has to. In your mind you still see it as a saviour for your relief, and yes it is a saviour in your mind, your brain needs it and there is no relenting up from this desire to have another drink.

If you try to stop, the feelings get so intense that there is nowhere to go but for another drink. It can wrack with unbelievable pain both physically and mentally. Somehow, in your own mind, your brain starts to drive you into a terrible, horrific madness. There are only two ways you can go now, there are no other choices. This is now D-day, the fear of a life without the booze seams totally out of the question. There is no other life but with alcohol, and inside there is a still a constant feeling of your friend in the bottle calling you like the devil itself. Believe me the devil can take many formats and thrives and relies on your downfall for its own gain, and it can only enter into your life in times of a low ebb, which it has already done, but to most people in this state of affairs the battle seems to have now been lost.

But I beg of you for your own salvation have faith at this time. A simple and maybe to you in this hour of desperate time an irrelevant thought. But, this is crunch time. You cannot live with it any more, there is no further hope for you if you do not find and have faith, faith in the God Almighty. Think to yourself of all the thousands of people in your situation that did not take on board faith, or they could not believe in the Higher Power, the Holy Spirit itself and are probably not alive to read this, but at this moment you *are* alive, I can only pray for you that the Holy Spirit and the love of God enters your body to rid you off this devil that is eating away inside you, and rest assured that if you also pray to God and seek Him with all your heart He will hear you and be by your side to relieve you of this terrible illness forever. Always hold on tightly to your faith, as in no way will the road ahead will be an easy one for you to regain your health, and maybe your family and your real friends. All that the devil in the bottle took away from you, to leave you on the very brink of death, degraded and despicable - a mere nothing in life.
There is now a way forward for you, with the Lord by your side and new friends to help and support you. Real friends.

In the following chapters, I myself who knows and understands all too well the problems and difficulties, will help you day-by-day to a totally new life. A life that you thought never existed without the bottle. New friends to be made, a whole new life that you could not believe was out there is now within your grasp. God wants us all to be happy, to be our true selves with integrity and some gentle pride in ourselves, but we must always have faith in the Lord for all of this to happen, it is not difficult. Throw away old cynicism. Be a new person. Do not forget I myself was in a worst state of this illness than you are at this present time, and I am still here with a new life and a loving feeling of peace without the booze. I have a new and positive life with new friends. If I can, so can you.

Coining to Terms - the Full Blown Alcoholic

My heart goes out to anybody that is in the lowest level of this illness; this terrible addiction that takes you into degradation and ignominious death. You cannot get any lower, in fact to many people in this terrible level of alcoholic addiction, the thought of another day is in itself a dreadful thought, a an even worse anticipation of a day to come.

You are now on the bottom rung of the ladder of your life and if you take one more step down that will be it it is the harsh reality of this addiction, the final degradation into death. If you are able to read this, you may still be fooling yourself It might already be a terrible situation, but the addiction is blinding you to just how close you are; even now you are degraded to a sub human level, despised by most of your friends and relatives. You may or not believe it, or may still not want to believe it, because the addiction in your very brain, in your own controlling mind is now completely controlled by the alcoholic addiction. It doesn't want you to stop. Your brain which controls your body doesn't want you to stop. It disregards all sense and all reason. Your whole body can go into convulsions and even panic attacks where you almost die at the remotest thought of no booze. Yes I know it's absolutely frightening. It's worse than being burned alive, to say the least. You may have little or no money, no concerns for food, the state you are living in, the degraded physical condition that you have become, or anything else, because every penny counts to buy even that one more can or bottle. It has now literally taken hold of your whole life. You no longer understand shame or what you are doing to yourself You have already disregarded your friends and family, probably stolen from them, pleaded with them until their pity for you has run dry. You at the bottom of being a recognisable human being; even shoplifting has become a way of life to maintain and fuel the addiction.

Probably by now food or other forms of sustenance is last thing on your mind because it would seem to be just a waste of money: money that could buy more booze. Somewhere in your addiction, the alcohol is still your friend. Ask yourself for a moment, and try to be honest with yourself,: is the devil in the bottle really a saviour, a friend to trust in? It's a very hard question to answer isn't it at this time?

I can feel you thinking up all sorts of excuses to yourself to justify why more booze is the best way. You will try and avoid the truth that there is no justification at all for your pitiful and by now terrible existence. You are inventing reasons, outlandish and stupid reasons to yourself Somewhere, deep inside you, you know it; that your whole life is being dictated to by the booze, that you are degraded, pitiful and dirty, probably not washing your clothes or even bathing yourself This, sadly is for too many the norm. Your home, if you still have it is an absolute and total mess, so by now you may be living on the street begging for money. Anything to somehow get more alcohol, or anything to ease the frightful effects of the alcoholic withdrawal.

Take it from me this cannot carry on, there is only one end. Please believe me that there is now nowhere to go, and I shudder at the time of writing this what you are experiencing so please do not think you are on your own, many people in this state are often admitted to hospital and its bloody awful to have a sudden no drink situation, that terrible withdrawal, **but a situation that maybe for the better if you can take it - and only you know the answer to that one.**

Depression is also a large part of the alcoholic's nature, perhaps fuelled by the alcohol in many ways. The more you get depressed the more you drink, the more you drink the more you get depressed so you need more drink to ease that increasing spiral. It is a no win situation to be involved in, you are probably dreading the morning dawn to some degree as depression is more intense in the morning and this again sets off the body for more and there is no way out except to surrender yourself to the booze. Booze seems to be the friend that stops the depression. So, for you, it's anything to take away the depression and intense frightening effects of withdrawals, of alcohol denial. Loneliness also is many a fearful situation. Your friends, even your drinking friends will probably be nowhere to be seen because you have already made yourself unwelcome by your requests for money or pleadings for them to buy you drinks.

By now even those that you have loved, your own family, even your own children may have also given up on you, there is now only one choice left to you if you do not want to be just another filthy, degraded pitiful pisshead creeping ever closer to being on the list of so many people that have died of this terrible illness. You in yourself are the only person that can bring forth a change and I know it's so hard to come to terms at the thought of no booze, it's absolutely frightening, but you know that you cannot carry on. There is no future in the direction you are now heading.

By reading this there is a way of changing and reversing the appalling state you are now in. For in this book of hope there is a light at the end of the tunnel; if you have faith, because your faith in the Lord Almighty will let Him hear your call, and you will find a way forward, to let the loving Holy Spirit enter your mind and body and in this way, rid yourself of this terrible degrading illness forever..

GIVING UP DAY BY DAY
A NEW BEGINNING
STEP BY STEP DAY
BY DAY

The Social Drinker

We have described the social drinker on page 30. As the term suggests, probably you are only drinking for entertainment in the midst of friends or for companionship with others. The way that the social media has evolved it may be a blind date, or an anniversary, at a wake, or just to celebrate just about anything really. Of course, even a couple of drinks always puts you at ease to talk more freely, to relax and take in the atmosphere of the event; and why not! If you are lucky enough to do this on a 'take it' or 'leave it' basis and have not strayed from that, then stay the same if you wish and enjoy your drink, and think how lucky you are to enjoy a drink for what it is.

However, there is a distinct difference between going to an event or the pub just for an occasional drink, and going for the alcoholic boost of the booze rather than the event itself. Always beware of using any social occasion just to have a drink. Of course many people feel out of place and sometimes scorned by others for having a soft drink, as if there is something wrong with you or you are driving for instance. Do not feel embarrassed by this or aware that you are not drinking alcohol, no one else really notices anyway.

There are different levels of social drinking which are bordering on the line of becoming a more regular drinker. This happens so slowly, sometimes over the years that you do not realize it yourself. There is only one way to really evaluate this and that is by thinking back two to five years ago to see the amount of booze you were drinking then. If you are just a social drinker it should be at the same level of non drinking and contained within special events of an occasional meal. If not, then you are at risk of becoming a regular drinker and so on.

Never feel that by stopping drinking alcohol altogether you are strange or will not fit in with others. In fact, it is quite the contrary. It is quite common for partners to notice one another's alcohol consumption, but it is not always easy for one to stop drinking or cut down while the other person is still drinking. Like most addictions, the one most addicted wants the other to join with them. All too often this causes immense friction between them. At this social stage of drinking it is quite easy to cut down or to give up completely. Going to the pub can be just a habit with only habitual "pub friends" to some degree and maybe you are lonesome and find comfort there. But there is a whole wide world out there to explore with new friends and a new outlook in life - just take that move into a different way of life. It really is not as difficult as you might think. There are countless clubs, without alcohol as an ingredient around in all communities. Don't spurn them. Try looking - going and introducing yourself until you end up finding and enjoying a new interest and new friends..

Your problem with alcohol is not really serious at all if you feel that the gain in friendship and relaxation after a hard days' work sometimes deserves a drink, then why not carry on and enjoy it for what it is supposed to be, no more than an occasional social drink.

THE REGULAR DRINKER

Any regular drinker, whether you admit it or not, is alcohol dependent to varying degrees of this illness.

There is quite a broad range from being at the lower scale to the higher scale of addiction and dependence. If you are anywhere within it the chances are that you like to get merry or even pissed on most days. That feeling of the first drink at the session is like nectar to you. You know you like it, your whole body likes it, as if total contentment sets in. Disregarding anything else in life, it has become your life, and to some, even their hourly rate of pay is measured in pints. Your way of life is constructed around a drink, if you think about it. For example, you probably know more about the price of booze than a loaf of bread. You are also spending most of your disposable income on the stuff, but in your mind it is fully justified. You would think that being dependent on the booze is like being dependent on the air we breathe. Alcohol is a friend to you, or seems to be.

Constant drinking during ones dinner hour with or without some sort of meal is also an indication of a growing problem becoming serious, which is probably getting worse if you then further enhance it with a drink when you get home or whenever you can get it. Some people, if there is not enough time to stay in the pub with other "pub friends" drinking, then they will drink a very strong beer, or a beer with a spirit chaser or whatever, to still receive the same amount of alcohol into their system quicker. The pretence of this being a social thing a jolly time with a friend is now gone.

Everybody is different as to what his or her body needs to find its level of contentment gained from the booze. There are warning signs like being irritable before being able to have a drink, being restlessness before the pub opens mainly on a Sunday, and the long wait till 12 o'clock or whatever time is imposed on you at work or by family commitments or restraints.

The final outcome list is endless and takes many formats, from marriage breakups, losing your home, hospitalisation because of ill health, to stealing and self degradation. It takes no prisoners, and even by reading this book is a way forward to yourself, and also maybe to

your family and close friends around you. They are truly concerned for your future welfare.

At this stage, it's a very daunting thought to have a life without booze, a whole way of addition that has become your life. If you use booze for depression, for example, although the booze actually makes it worse in real terms, it's not easy to even comprehend your saviour friend in the bottle, is given up and gone. This is, you feel your safety net of life. How awful it feels to not only suffer from the withdrawals of your friend in the bottle, but to go through the turmoil you would then be facing.

But. you will not be facing it on your own day by day. **Together** we will become united in pushing away your fears and supporting you through the horrible ill feelings of denial of the booze. Acute loneliness for some is the same. You have, whether you fully realise it or not, bee using the booze to help eradicate this feeling of being lonely and inadequate. But, the booze has reduced you from friends and has just increased your loneliness and proved to others an inadequacy.

There is hope and there is a light at the end of the tunnel, however far it may be, and that hope is worth grasping and holding onto tightly as you can.

I feel for you and believe me that it is probably the booze making you lonely and increasing your depression. You are lonely because you were shy, and haven't felt able to take steps into finding new friends. You probably do not get involved in any other social events to even try to make new friends. Because of this, you have got yourself in an alcoholic sustained hellhole. Believe me, there is a new life out there, much more interesting and exciting and satisfying than just sitting indoors getting pissed or in the comer of a bar sinking slowly into an abyss. And if the truth's known, most of the others there are on exactly the same road as you, and are no help to you whatsoever.

All sorts of problems make us drink too much, but have you ever thought to yourself how non-drinkers feel? Do you assume that they have no problems at all? Yes, it really brings home to you now that you are caught up by the devil in the bottle, using any way to tempt you into further alcoholism. Whatever your own specific reasons for concern are for your alcoholism, there is a way forward. It's not going to be easy but it will be easier than being a full-blown alcie. Consider yourself lucky to some degree that there is a chance to regain maybe your job and your family that your illness and addiction has caused all the ill-feeling that you have put on them. You cannot change the past but you can change the future - a future of love and hope.

Others may still feel concerned to be close to you again, but this can again be rekindled with the help of the love of Christ. Please do not dismiss the love and the care that the Holy Spirit can give you to eradicate the devil in the bottle forever. The road ahead is not easy, but, believe me at all times have faith. Faith in Jesus Christ Himself and also faith in your own self to ease the way forward to a much better life is what you want; a new life and a new beginning without the booze.

When to give up

There is only one time to give up and the time unfortunately for you is **today.** Do not deceive yourself in any way by inventing excuses to justify another day or a future date, as that will never come because you will only find some other problem in your life to carry on drinking when all the time it's the drinking that is causing all the problems. The problems in your life will not go away instantly and you must be aware constantly of all the grief that the **booze** has caused you. This will always enhance your will to survive without it, especially in the first few weeks of denial of your so-called friend. Please say to yourself, now **today's the day.** It's a bloody awful decision to make but always have it in your head that you are so lucky to not be a full-blown alkie yet, with even more serious withdrawals to contend with.

That last sentence will become very apparent to you so do not forget it at all cost. So let's assume that the day of reckoning has arrived, not just for you, but maybe the day of reckoning for others in the Home. For instance, maybe your loving wife will regain the lost love for you or vice versa, or indeed the both of you may have the same drinking problem and together help each other in coming to terms with the day to give up. If however, only one in the relationship can see the light, it is obviously more difficult for the other to continue denial of the booze, but that is a personal choice however difficult. Keep to the long road ahead for your own sake. Do not keep the fact that you are about to give up from your family or friends either, as they will be more understanding in your day-by-day achievements. Some will be totally jealous or envious by your future success. Forget also all the pundits, the know it all types, who sneeringly dismiss you, who have deemed you just a complete piss head and useless junk which then in depression, feeling there is nothing else for you, tempts you to just carry on boozing. That's only their way of loosening you from their fold that also justifies their own pathetic existence. In most cases they will drop you like a stone anyway, showing you that they are not really the friends you had thought them in your earlier "pubbing days".. They are only the same as the so-called friend in the pub that you are now, if you want it, going to lose forever for a real and better life with true friends, all attainable with help and sincere understanding in the following chapters.

Day One Of Giving Up For The Regular Drinker

Let us assume it's the morning of the new beginning and you do not drink first thing, so your first day ahead of no booze has not really started yet in your mind or body, but of course as the day wears on the craving will become more intense. Perhaps, normally at the time you would start to drink - say mid or late morning to lunchtime session, or again in the evening session. The severity of denial will always be linked to the level of your past intake at the given time of your normal top-up. That is to say, the more dependent you were (the more you drank), the worse the withdrawals will be from one person to another. However, nobody should assume that if you are, say in a self-help group for example, they feel any better or worse than someone else, it's bloody awful for anybody to go through. Have the compassion to relate to others in the way they feel to which, in turn, will help you. It is also an advantage to go to a meeting at the Alcoholics Anonymous - usually referred to as the A A - to see how you get on. There you can easily relate to others and they to you, which is very comforting. Take it from me, it can become a very lonely, hazardous place to be doing this on your own. Don't be frightened to take all the help you can, from wherever its offered - **just fight against returning to take it from the bottle.**

However, this is your first day of denial, the first symptoms will probably be restlessness, not being able to sit still, walking around the room; sitting and rubbing your hands together or your feet; possibly having profuse sweating and a total lack of concentration, linked with a level of fear; causing acute anxiety similar to being in a dentists' chair; all of these and more to come. **But, have faith. This is the devil in the bottle calling for you to give in.**

"Another drink will take all of these horrendous symptoms away" and *"what real harm is there in Just one drink"* is what you will be hearing now in your head, very persuasive That drink is precisely all you are thinking about - you need to find relief - and it is so simple to give in to these devils' calls. Your own mind is trying to turn you back to the alcohol and an ultimate degrading and hideous end with death.
If you are a smoker it's not unusual for you to chain smoke, increasingly, but without real purpose or any enjoyment. So what! Anything that seems

to help eradicate some of the symptoms is fine for a while. Strong coffee will also help to give you some sort of buzz. If you were a beer drinker it is also very helpful to drink lots of soft drinks to fill the stomach with fluid to somehow decoy the system of capacity within it. All these ways to some degree help, but the only person who counts really is you. You need to hang on, somehow, to that small inner core, your inner strength to resist the devil in your own mind. The devil in your mind that is so addicted that it doesn't care about you, how it will eventually drag you down to a sub-human, degraded level before eventually killing you.

As hard and as far away that this may seem, an intense loneliness can be present to some, as the highlight of your day may have been chatting to people in the bottle, or drinking the day away on your own using the booze to get out of life and into your own world for a while, to eradicate loneliness only to find it worse the day after. You know it's true, so look at each passing hour without the booze as a blessing. A blessing, small though it seems at first, but a blessing that will grow and find strength and give you survival, friends and a new and fulfilling life. A new life.

Struggle and hold on. Do not be at all tempted to give in, as this first day of denial will bring spontaneous strong urges to have a drink. Never think to yourself that just one drink will be ok and expect it to be just that. It's over for you if you think you are in control of your future intake. It is impossible for any regular drinker of the past to control his or her future if you drink at all. It's over! Do not deceive yourself in any way. The power of denial will drum up all sorts of mindless ideas. *'I will drink a weak beer; in future I will not go out as much; I will do this; I will do that.'* Totally dismiss all of these negative thoughts that are being created by the addicted part of your mind telling your body to actually deceive itself into having a drink again. To you, all these thoughts seem very real, very strong, **but do not give in to them. Have faith! Have faith in your true self.**

If you are lucky enough to have someone at your side during this terrible ordeal of withdrawal, to listen to all sorts of rubbish you may come up with, and to hold you firm, you are fortunate. It is not uncommon to have moments of tears or laughter after the worst moments - or a mixture at the same time. Yes, you could be hallucinating because your body is crying out for more booze. Your body has become used to operating as best it could to the poisoning by alcohol. It may be that you are at work and you used to always have a few beers at dinnertime; again a denial will probably cause a total lack of concentration on your everyday tasks, causing absolute mayhem in your mind.

Believe it or not, keeping busy and trying hard in what you do, however hard it may seem to you, is the way forward. As this is your first day of a new life without booze, it will be hard, probably very hard, but do not falter. Forget your work colleagues. Do not feel stupid or even guilty that you are not with them either. It's you and you alone who matters from now on and it's only you who can overcome the desires of this terrible addiction.
So, let's assume that you have missed your dinner time session and you are back on the job. Congratulate yourself although you probably feel bloody awful. **You managed it!** It's the first step on a journey that becomes better and better as a new life slowly opens up - almost like discovering a new world. A new world which will come into reality as each day passes without the poison of alcohol.

Now, on leaving work it would be so easy to give in on the way home, as by now the withdrawals are taking a stronger hold on you. Again and again, your own mind, your own brain is trying to tempt you to take just one - what would just one hurt? But, just one will take you skittering and sliding down again. Down towards the pit of sub-life. Again force yourself to go straight home. You have come this far - see it through. Summon up all your resolve, all your strength. If at all possible, going to bed early and trying to sleep is a good idea as by doing so gives you a break from the temptations of the withdrawals.

Do not think that your life will ever be the same. Your life is changing. New horizons, perhaps now only dimly seen, but they are there. Those new horizons will bring a new and incredibly better life. Courage! Keep positive and take one day at a time. Every day in every way the symptoms, the withdrawal pains and temptations will lessen, your past life will not be so important to you because as the weeks go by a whole new life will emerge.

There may be new friends to meet at a different location than the pub, new friends, new ideas in your life to make a complete change in your social life as well. Try to look forward to this. It's not magic, it's not instant, but it is happening, slowly but surely as each alcohol free day passes. It's not easy but you must. There is a whole big wide world out there that you have completely missed for years because of your addiction. However, you have not had a drink today. This day you will always remember as a godsend, although it does not feel like it at the present time as the poisoned part of your brain tries endlessly to pervert you back into just one drink, to start again the ways of self destruction and degradation..

You probably have periods where you still feel bloody awful and that's not surprising. Your whole body is by now craving for the booze. Shaking, sweats, convulsions, being irritable and bad tempered - this is an absolutely agonizing period as you shake off the effects of the poison, and this may make life with you difficult as well. Try to be tolerant to them, just as they try to be tolerant to you. This is not an easy time for you, nor for those around you. Be as kind as you can, although this is not easy.

Do not give in and do not be tempted in any way of the devil's call for drink, however small. The more you abstain the greater the hardship will be because the devil in the poisoned part of your brain will push you farther and further in the hope that you will give in. Do not now waste your efforts. Do not succumb to the devil for you have not had a drink all day and evening. Just go to bed, try to sleep. It is also not uncommon to wake during the night, as the body will try all sorts of tricks to tempt you.

Have faith. Have faith in you. You CAN do this. Just let your true self, the part of you able to fight for survival hang on with resolve. It will become more tolerable in a few days. Every day in every way is a major step forward. Congratulate yourself that you have handled a working day and evening. It is an enormous achievement.

However, the weekend will arrive. And when this comes your life can now seem empty. You are missing the weekend boozing, whether with "pub friends" or sitting outside on a hot summer's day with an ice-cold beer, or having friends around for a Barbie or whatever you do, life without these things which include alcohol, seem to now have no meaning to you. This is a tough time, but however you feel, whatever the temptations, hang on and have faith in that inner strength that got you started back onto a new and better life. **Have faith..**

The depressions may set in and you may feel jealous or very envious that others are getting merry and enjoying themselves. It's not very inspiring to oneself being sober and getting involved in their conversation or pissed up behaviour. You now know how other people looked at you in your pissed up past. But, it is now a past. You have taken that amazingly important first steps.

In the present you will start to see yourself gradually drifting away from the sort of leisure events and also the dwindling invitations that used to come your way. Some people give up ringing you for different reasons. For example, some feel guilty drinking in your presence, some may feel responsible for a restart in your addiction, or you quite simply do not fit in with the crowd anymore. It's quite strange how pissed up people to some degree, subconsciously are aware of your sober presence and give you a wide berth. Look on this as a subtle benefit. They are not, and probably never were true friends.

What the hell does it matter! You have lost nothing, and if the truth be known, they
know you have gained everything they themselves cannot, or have not yet managed to
gain, which is to be a part of that new and better life..
They still can see no further than the bottom of a glass.
They, sadly, still listen to the poisoned, addicted part of their brain.

By now slowly taking each day without booze, life can seem somewhat grey, dismal or boring and seriously depressing at times, and you may have feelings that cannot see a new future. But it is there. It really is. Your depressions and failure of belief is more of your poisoned part of your own brain. More illusions to try and pervert you back to a drink. However, there **is** a big future coming your way. It's only that you have not had enough time to adjust to a new way of life yet. Perhaps you cannot yet look around yourself to see your slow but steady gain. No-one can change years of alcoholism overnight, but just look at what you have accomplished overnight or over a week. It is really something that most cannot, as yet manage to change. Being sober day by day; that is an amazing achievement in the defeating of a terrible and pernicious addictive poison by anyone's standards.

Think back in the book and relate to me having been far worse than you; aren't you lucky that by being only alcohol dependent and not further down the slippery slope into degradation and at death's door like myself? Be glad that you can survive and reconstruct a new life, a better life, and that your withdrawals are, luckily, even if they are terrible to you now, they £ire from what they could be only mediocre. Could you, after experiencing your demonised level of withdrawal, even risk going back on the piss? Could you honestly endure it? The answer is probably no, **so do not ever think as the months go by that you can have even one drink or that the devil in the bottle has gone away.**

The poison is and will always remain addictive for you. The devil in the bottle, is always waiting for you to think you are fine after a few months; that you can control your drinking, with maybe just a small sip, but just that will make you start again. **Do not at any cost deceive yourself! This is a danger time.**

It is the time so many, slip, slide and tumble back into an even worse condition.

Most of the people who start boozing again after denial, will in days be back much and worse than before. It is as if your body is making up for lost time. The defence you started, has collapsed and the addictive poison of alcohol has won, and celebrates by taking you further down the road of degradation and death.

When I was there, there were some people at the AA meetings who described how they thought they could handle only half a beer, but within days they were pissed up totally, and always worse than before. They had to go through more serious, more painful and more terrible withdrawals yet again, and this time with a weakened belief in their capability to win.

Think to yourself again at this moment - could you go through withdrawals again. The answer is definitely NO! Very few people get a second chance and I beg of you to stay the way you are, however hard the road ahead may seem. Stay alcohol free. Live a life.

There will be many times of feeling low and the following words are very true and can be very powerful and useful in times of need:

GOD.
GRANT ME THE SERENITY TO ACCEPT THE THINGS I CANNOT CHANGE, AND COURAGE TO CHANGE THE THINGS I CAN AND THE WISDOM TO KNOW THE DIFFERENCE

Think carefully on the meaning. These loving words at times were also my saviour as they will be yours. Please do not give in to the devil as the love of Jesus Christ is at your side. If you take on in your heart the love of Christ and in your life the Holy Spirit, the devil will be afraid. The love and power of Jesus Christ always will override the devil's evil ways.

If you are a Christian you will already be aware of the above, and for those who are not practicing Christians, or of another faith, think carefully before making the wrong judgment and sliding back into drink, look for a greater power, a heavenly faith. Look back in the book of my true-life story when the Lord came into my life at nearly my time of death, to save me for a future. You too will have a future.

I cannot express how much I feel for those who are at this moment suffering from this terrible addiction and the illnesses it causes. All alcohol eventually brings is just that -illness and a slide into degradation and further into a sub human state and death.

I pray that their family and close friends will stand by them. If they are reading this book, please do not give up on them. If they have abused or mistreated you, remember it's only the poison within the shell of the loving person you used to know.
In most cases the inner heart is still there. It is impossible to really know from the outside looking in, the level of hell that is in one's body. You would have to encounter it yourself to fully understand how ill one feels. Be as patient as you can be in their first few months of being clean. It is very hard probably for you also to have to put up with very quick mood swings or a bad temper. It would be totally unreasonable to expect anything different really. Patience and compassion is needed. It does get better and better.

As this chapter of the book is for the very concerned *regular drinker* with problems, in times of temptation or distress, please read on and take in the absolutely frightening facts of being a *full blown alkie* that you will become if you do not take stock of yourself now. Some parts of the last chapter may be offensive to you. I sincerely hope that, for your own sake, you never get to the level of the full-blown addition riddled alkie.

Helping And Understanding The Full Blown Alkie

It never ceases to amaze me that all the problems associated with smoking seem to override the more serious issue of alcohol abuse. Alcohol abuse is so much more serious, causing social and health problems for the immediate circle of friends and family and by its costs, the whole community. Much more so than just lighting a cigarette. Has smoking ever caused anyone really to end up in prison or caused violence and family break-ups. Yes, it can lead to death and serious health conditions, even death? Smoking is in no way as damaging to friends and family and all of society.

How many people are at this present time in prison for smoking tobacco related crimes? Now, look at the same for those addicted or just hinging on alcohol. You think about it yourself for a moment. We go into our supermarket and any other store, for that matter, and are not allowed to even see cigarettes on sale. But of course it's fine to see rows and rows of booze - beers, ciders, wines and spirits openly displayed in as tempting a manner as possible.

I often wonder what planet the powers that be are on. It is little wonder really that our country is having the increasing, huge drink related problems that has evolved, and we are told will become ever worse as the years evolve to show wasted liver problems and increasing numbers of alcoholics within our society. Wherever you go, from a garage to every corner shop in the country, it stares you in the face. Little wonder that even school children are at risk. We are all at risk. Life itself seems to revolve around booze without any concern for the victims. Booze slowly, day-by-day, takes yet more and more lives.

On life's journey, from a young age, there is no way of knowing that one day thousands of us will die from being a full blown alkies. The social media seems to push this very serious illness to one side as you are just simply branded a piss head. Any non-drinker will probably assume you just like to get pissed or you even do it for the taste. What really pisses me off is that most think that you have always been a waster and to some degree that is all you have ever been. How naive can some people be, that even the medical profession looks down on you, although it can affect a tramp to an eminent surgeon or company director, manager or skilled worker. It takes no prisoners in all classes of professions.

The point that I am making is that if you have, in your family, friends or anyone else who is in the final stages of this illness, please stand by them. God himself only knows how awful this highly addictive illness is.

That lovely person that you once married for example, now a complete wasting away mess, or it could be your own mother or father or son or daughter. There seems no way of knowing what it is that some become addicted, whilst others do not.

I cannot tell you any other greater feeling than it would be to have any loved one back at your side from a terrible alcoholic addiction. Back to yourself in the way that loving person you loved used to be. **It is possible.**

I'm here to write it that it is possible to regain a faith, with help into life once more. I am proof in life alone that there is a chance for your loved one to rid his or herself off the hellish addiction which degrades and eventually slides into death.

You may have tried so many times to help them before, and you are possibly now at breaking point yourself, I actually believe that any body's life, including the sad victim is worth saving with love and compassion. Some of you may have possibly been hurt so much by the boozed up victim that you may not care for what happens to them at all. But, basic humanity means it is impossible to not care for them somewhere, even if you've given up in despair.

I can understand that, but please ask yourself a question before making any judgement. Can you live your life with their death on your shoulders? That seems unfair, but it is not to say that any friend or relative is guilty of neglect that allows the alcohol victim to slide to death. If you have done all you can do and have had faith and the victim has had no faith, there probably is no hope at all, for without faith none of us has anything.

No one really, in my mind can understand the addicted victims total dilemma, not even the medical profession, unless they have experienced it themselves and many have come back from the grave from this illness. Many, probably most alcoholic victims are totally ill-treated by all the others in society because it seems totally self inflicted. Which is in a way, but the random, fickle finger of fate that makes one person sink into addiction, and not another makes it really a problem that cannot be predicted. Why therefore do they take that utter most stupid view that you like being what you are, or that it was entirely your fault? You have, after all, initially just joined in to the socially accepted normal behaviour..

They must be totally brain dead to assume that any totally emancipated, intelligent alcoholic addicted person likes to be the way they are, I do understand that the alcoholic addiction does make our behaviour very difficult, and sometimes a waste of time because of recession, but and understanding with compassion would surely mean more sense and the likelihood of more being saved. I have meet some very nasty nurses in my unfortunate stay in hospital with this illness and I do believe that if it was not for a few very caring nurses, that also looked after me with understanding and compassion, often in their own time, I doubt very much that I would have, with God's help survived to help others in their darkest hours of need. I am writing all of this to you, yes **you** as possibly by reading this I hope that you do not give up on anybody that is close to you, friend or family by your side who at this present time is at the final stage of the terrible addictive illness. Help, please, however faraway this ultimate ending may seem to you at the present time.

I praise myself, that very much with God's help that I have helped and totally cured others, to completely eradicate them from this awful illness and allow them to resume their past life, or create a new life back to normal or even to have found a much better life within the Christian faith.

The full blown alkie has perhaps only you now. Would anybody let an animal suffer in this way? Of course not, so its surely not right that, as I speak to you, one human to another lets some of our society actually rot away from this illness just because they are wrongly deemed a pisshead, a person of no importance, when they are gravely ill for Christ's sake. II find it difficult to write how I feel. How I feel that the chance of a person being capable of alcohol or any other type of addiction should be blamed for it. Drugs, perhaps one can argue it is a known choice, but alcohol is a socially used medium for most celebrations, with meals or social gatherings.

Think back in the book when 1 described that the few people at the AA meetings who like myself were at deaths door experienced and who gained the same spiritual healing by God himself, the fact that just these very few people including myself were saved when thousands of others were not, just because we were able to take and get strength within the faith. God as we all should know is said to work in strange ways, and I can hear you saying to yourself, why does God not step in and save everybody, it is off-course the simple fact that anybody that has a Christian faith in the God Almighty will always override the devil. It is the devil that always thrives in our demise. In this case the devil is in the bottle and has used alcohol to bring your life and the unfortunate victims around you to descend into a life in total disarray and increasing misery. The power and depth of love of God will always eradicate the devil forever, and let you and your loved ones to be free of this all the side effects of this horrific addictive illness forever. It is such a relief to know that any Christian with faith cannot be afraid of the devil because with faith in The Almighty God, the devil is totally afraid of you.

I sincerely hope that after reading this chapter of helping and understanding a full blown alkie, you will find in your heart the ability to be linked closely with faith in God so that your prayers will be answered, and the person that you almost gave up on is now back at your loving side, it's all worth it, however hard or unforgiving you may feel at this present time words can say no more. It's now up to you and in the last chapter of Freedom from Hell, I hope that now you and the victim will have a much better understanding and a way forward for ever.

Freedom from Hell

You may or not be too ill to read this or even understand this final chapter, and if not I sincerely hope that help is at hand for you to bring you the message so you can understand it. It's quite possible you may be in hospital, or in a mental institution or similar clinic, or festering away on your own. You are possibly now on the bottom rung of the ladder. You have tried so hard to give up, probably finding it harder and harder and to no avail. It all seems so impossible for you, and it may be impossible for you. Right now as much as it hurts, you may feel that it's all over. You feel that you cannot get any lower; there is no lower a human being can get, you are immensely frightened, frightened by the past, and more so by the diminishing future, the only result can now be death. It may well be that the fear of the denial of the booze outweighs the will to survive in a world where booze is all around you. A constant and probably irresistible temptation.

You can be free.! There is a way forward, that is perhaps right now at this present time seemingly just out of reach, your body is absolutely on fire with awesome, terrible wracking withdrawals, feeling sick and at times semi-conscious, you are drifting away, in fact a perfectly good person, just rotting away.

I beg of you, do not give in. It's all too easy to do that. Your overall, addicted and poisoned mind is probably saying to you give up. Yes? And I know too well that feeling of not being able to cope with all this for another minute. It's just too awesome to cope with anymore. Yes, it is unimaginable for anyone to cope with this now D-day has arrived. That also brings about the fact that you feel that you cannot live without a drink and you are beginning to truly understand that you will not be able to live much longer with it. If you are at a place where you cannot get your hands on another drink, however much your own addicted mind might try to resist the fact, then that's the start of the beginning. You have no choice in the matter. So use this as a milestone with no going back, and if you are at home with booze in the house pour it down the sink, or if you are too ill to move, resist feelings against, ask someone to do this for you if possible, either way it will create fear in yourself, fear of those terrible withdrawals. It is probably the fear of the terrible effects of the withdrawals that fuels the most fear. It's like a ball running down a hill, the more speed it gains, bumping and bouncing out of control, the more the anguish. Yes, you are at this moment in a no win situation, you may even be sleeping rough, cold and very weak with no friends or relatives to call upon, or in your room that's probably like a pigsty.. If this is the case or you are in the worst situation. May those who can help, find you in time, my sincere advise is somehow get to A&E, in a hospital, if you are now totally emancipated and past caring for yourself, that is your only choice, once there, hopefully you will be admitted and given care for your own welfare. It's bloody hard decision to make the thought of no booze and no fags, the two withdrawals are an awesome thought for you, but there is now no other choice. You will hopefully now have a warm, clean bed and be cared for. The detox pills do work to some degree to assist the uncontrollable shaking and spewing. If a friend is with you they should help you to achieve all of this. For your own sake, it's a lot easier to give yourself maybe your last chance whilst in hospital as there is no way of having a drink and set yourself back on the way to becoming sub-human, degraded and ultimately dead.

If you are at home or on the street without any help there is only one way out for you to go, and that is to pray for God to step into your darkest hour and save you from this awesome existence, you must have faith. I look back on the awfulness that might have been my own life if the God Almighty had not entered into my darkest hour. I would have been dead long ago. You too can rid yourself of this alcoholic addiction. You must, by now know in your heart that you would give anything to be the person you once was, or a new person with a new life clear of alcohol and all it can do to destroy the very essence of yourself From this moment in your life pray to God that you can give up, pray to God to help you to tolerate the coming days of unimaginable effects of the withdrawals.

Every day in every way, slowly your mind and body will improve, everyday is a start. Take every day as a part of a new beginning, yes even with possibly the help of a higher being, your God's help, you will feel awful and the days ahead can seem sometimes to have no meaning, you will begin to know that it's your past that has had no meaning, and looking to the future has not yet had the chance to give you a new meaning. But it will, and that new meaning will be you, you without the need and addictive and corrosive additive of alcohol.

But a new life will evolve in you, in the early days of withdrawals, however hard and so far away that may seem, have faith, there are times looking back myself when I almost gave in but the Lord was with me as He will be with you if you have faith. I am not brainwashing you into thinking that the future life of no booze is a bed of roses either, it will never be if you do not find peace, a true peace within yourself. It's a feeling that you cannot buy or borrow or even think of as everybody's level and conception of tranquil peace is so different and immensely important to the individual.

But to start and enjoy a whole new life, one must first get one's health back and depending how ill you are, the longer it will take, it is not unusual to take up to 3 years for the body to get back all of your wasted muscle tissue and back in trim, and all of system replenished with vitamins that the alcohol has totally dissolved away from your possibly years of alcohol abuse. Your mind will have suffered and you will be suffering probably from post traumatic stress disorder as well, in anyway all of these aftermath symptoms are in themselves all a part of our new life, so do not be put off from your way forward. Even if you are reading this at a point of no return in your mind, day by day the withdrawals will very slowly decrease. However, sometimes it's not unusual for ones level of withdrawal to take a steep drive down hill again, and all I can say is, that from my own experience stay with the new beginnings. Have faith. You will have intermittent ups and downs, but rest assured that after a very bad down, for some reason you go up to a higher level of up. So do not let those days of total gloom sway you from your given goal. Always think to yourself, however hard it maybe, that now possibly you are making some headway. It is not always apparent. You might feel it is not always possible at the time of the down moments when you are feeling like the devil is prowling around, winning and tempting you and further arousing your thoughts of just one more drink. But, that is the way to the slide into complete self-destruct. Never give in. You have come so far now. Give yourself praise, it may now have been a week or may be more that you have been in denial. Difficult to see perhaps, but already you are winning.
Your whole body has a feeling of total emptiness, sickeningly deep depressions and possible loneliness, and confused about everyday living. I know that feeling all too well myself, it is absolutely impossible in these early days of denial to even concentrate on anything. Despair is always only just a whisker away.

It's not you as a person that is hugely guilty of all of this, it's your body that's confused by the lack of the booze. Your poisoned mind and body is still crying out loud for alcohol. But, by now you will begin to realise that it is possible for you to be in charge. That the real you is capable of rising up and defeating the poison of the alcoholic addiction. This is where you make sure that the real you is in charge of your mind and body, however hard they try to combine to push you into giving in. In these times of insecurity and confusion think back to day one of the denial and ask yourself could you now repeat that most terrible day of your life again? Could anybody put up with those intolerable feelings again? There is only one answer to that question and that's **"No way**! The fear of this will surely make you even more positive to carry on towards a new life, from the way forward that you are now travelling. It's quite like being burned once is the learning curve. Who in their right mind would do it all again? Do you really think now that you could go back to the way you were?

You have now succeeded in getting over the past few weeks, whether you are in hospital or being looked after by friends etc etc., or you may have even been on your *own,* if that was the case I can only sympathise with you, it's all a bloody nightmare where ever you've been, but on your own you have been a miracle. The best way forward now is to start eating. That can be quite a problem for some of us, the very thought of food can at times make you feel sick. If this is the case try eating little and often; small portions of scrambled egg for example, and / or a spoonful of honey is a light and easy to keep down, yet nutritional and easily digested food. Perhaps slowly introducing simple soups for a hot food choice. Try to drink as much fluid as possible, whether water, lemonades, tea and coffee, and in general gradually day by day improving the menu to suit the improvement of your own wellbeing. Possibly, your personal hygiene has suffered during your worst days, do not let this continue. Start a regime of good personal hygiene, it is not at all easy and sometimes downright impossible at times, especially if you are suffering from inward depression at the same time, and there will be periods of deep depression from time to time and in these moments its nigh on impossible to see a way forward, let alone washing and cleaning teeth etc.. But, this is normal, it will pass so do not feel that you are a waster or inadequate. You are not. You are coming out of one of the worst addictions and you are doing it by your own will. You have come this far and this is a real achievement in itself

It's also very important to try to keep up ones self-esteem and pride in yourself daily. You, and really only you can take pride in your denial of the booze. The AA at this time can be very reassuring, and I found that by being around others in the same predicament really can help you to also understand that you are not the only person to be living out this illness. Look at you now, you are slowly building up your inner strength and your morale. You have now the right to say to others that you are not an alcoholic, and take pride in yourself to say **"I am a recovering alcoholic"** and that is such an achievement by any ones standards, so you must feel justifiably proud of it.

You also owe it to yourself that you may have proved you to all of your past alcoholic so called friends, that they were wrong. Very wrong. To some that had previously branded you as a total waster, including some in the medical profession, that yes you are special *and* by having faith in yourself, and more so the inner most help from the Holy Spirit, look now that you are set for a new beginning. As for my part, looking back at myself to when I was at deaths door, I realise what a miracle and blessing my life now is. You really have to been through this awesome scenario of alcoholic addiction to have a full understanding of the love and healing powers of God himself that saved you for a great future, and there is a future for you. Also be aware that the devil is always hovering around you waiting for the slightest chance to be again your downfall, life is life and it would be so wrong to fill your head that all will be well all the way through life's incredible journey but by having faith you will always resist the temptations to drink and by so doing, overpower the devil that once again would absolutely relish you having another drop of alcohol and climb again onto that slippery slide down to hell. Always have these words to hand in your mind, or write it down to read to yourself in times of stress, **IF I DON'T PICKUP THE FIRST GLASS THEN I CANNOT GET PISSED.**

Also do not assume that in the early months of being a new recovering alcoholic that all of the distress that you may have ever had or caused will go away overnight. Although many will congratulate you on your present success, there will be some who will always say a leopard doesn't change its spots, and if you have just one little sip, they will be right, but with time your loved ones and former friends will actually be proud of your achievements, stay by the long road ahead and take each day as it comes. It is not a race so be tolerant with yourself you cannot run if you cannot walk, remember it took me 3 years to regain my strength alone and longer to repair the mental damage. Even God himself waited for the right time to call me to his house as he was also aware of my physical and mental situation to lead me to a whole new life. A new life that even before being a full blown alkie I did not know existed. Being saved by the Lord himself and the contentment of peace and tranquillity and new friends in the Christian faith that welcomed me with open arms, I and I alone can be eternally grateful, for all of this to happen against all odds, and it is over 8 years now that I have not had a drink, furthermore it has not even upset my social life one bit. I can actually go out to a pub to enjoy myself with friends with no thought in my mind of any intention of downing a beer, you too having faith in me will make yourself a much more positive person, and that will make others around you to be proud of you once again. If there are any doubting Thomas's out there then I and you alone will have proved them all wrong, furthermore I will and can only pray for any of you that are at this present time still a full blow alkie, and my sincere heart goes out to you for the intense suffering that you are enduring and your friends and family, and in times of stress learn and read the following

Lord, Help me to remember that nothing is going to happen
to me today That you and I can't handle together

Divine Intervention

The contents of this very moving book will help anyone in any stage of this terrible illness to give-up the booze forever, and like myself embark on a whole new life without the bottle for a life you may not have known existed other than your hellhole you are now in.

I sincerely hope that this very down to earth book will be your saviour and if any of the contents helps you, then I do not care if it offends others. I am thankful if I have helped you, and that I have helped you towards your new life, and hopefully helped you to come to terms with your new life. God bless.

N/B: Some of the proceeds of this book will go to help suffering alcoholics to see the light.

THE END.

And now what do I do? I Now Live

PS: Also a very big thank you to Juliette the greatest love in my life who inspired me to write this very moving and true book and stood by my side in times of uncertainty.

This compelling and true life story of the author taking you through a very troubled life to which led him to be a full blown alcoholic with only days to live to survive this awesome illness, by way of a very powerful spiritual happening.

<u>Special thanks to Alcoholics Anonymous for all there support in helping 1000s of people with this awesome addiction and illness</u>

Follow the continuation of my life in
The Drinkers Nightmare
(The Aftermath)
volume 2
Life goes on !

Made in the USA
Charleston, SC
28 December 2015